A Treasury of Texas Trivia

Bill Cannon

Republic of Texas Press

Library of Congress Cataloging-in-Publication Data

Cannon, Bill.
  A treasury of Texas trivia / Bill Cannon.
      p.   cm.
  Includes Index.
  ISBN 1-55622-526-1 (pb)
  1. Texas—Miscellanea. 2. Texas—Anecdotes. I. Title.
F386.6.C36   1996
976.4—dc10   96-40199
                                CIP

ISBN 1-55622-526-1
10 9 8 7 6 5 4 3 2 1
9701

All inquiries for volume purchases of this book should be addressed to Wordware Publishing, Inc., at 1506 Capital Avenue, Plano, Texas 75074. Telephone inquiries may be made by calling:

(972) 423-0090

Contents

The origin of Texas barbeque • the curse of the
courthouse clock • Texas' "Loch Ness Monster" • battle
named for a saint • the Black Bean Death Warrant • the
XIT Ranch • Oscar • the Yellow Rose of Texas • "Old
Rip" • Texas A&M's "12th man" • "Bevo" • Jim Bowie
and Dracula • Christopher Columbus and the jalapeno! •
"red light district" • "field of Cadillacs" • "bury the
hatchet" • the *Hindenburg* disaster • Texas fire bombed •
unusual cash crop • Langtry, Texas • William Marsh Rice
murdered • Santa Claus wounded in gun battle • Chapita
Rodriguez ghost's curse • seven flags over Texas? •
extra-terrestrial contacts in Texas • hogs discovered oil
field • ghost light of Bragg Road • Marfa lights • "neutral
area" • the wet town that dried up! • the "woman in
blue" • town ruled by walking cane • gunman's victim
helped bury himself • Waterloo • Highway 80 • Big
Spring • Texas navy • "gringo" • King Ranch • great
crash near Crush • Cuero • who's buried in Sam Bass's
grave? • the "car-barn convention" • "Texas-leaguer" •
Winchester Quarantine • wooden rails • Marshall • San
Elizaria • Stetson hat • streets paved with gold •
cowhands killed for singing • Chrysler's Dodge Texan •
John Wilkes Booth • the "Lost Battalion" • school for
one student • Mexico's chance to reclaim Texas •

Contents

People 89

Firsts 121

Man River" • movie filmed about the Battle of the Alamo • surgical operation • patent for processing condensed milk • chili powder • "king maker" • mass parachute drop • air passenger service • marriage ceremony • airplane used by military • airmail • automobile air conditioning • use of crude oil • oil well • hospital ship

Dedication

I fondly dedicate this book to my friend Jaan
McCoy of Dallas radio station KAAM-620
AM. Jaan has done so much through his radio
program *The Breakfast Club* to re-educate
those of us fortunate enough to be born in
the great state of Texas and to introduce
Texas to those less fortunate!

Foreword

Of all the wonderful things I have learned while putting together this collection of Texas trivia, the one thing I have most emphatically learned is that this book cannot ever be finished! One can only take a breather. As large as Texas is, and as diversified as its cultures are, there are far too many anecdotal and apocryphal stories which could be included, making a project such as this unending. Hopefully this offering will inspire readers to delve deeper into this "treasure chest" we call Texas history and lore for other gems to further enhance this glorious crown we call Texas!

Acknowledgments

There is no better place than at the beginning of a book such as this to pay tribute to those people who were so instrumental in bringing this collection of trivia items together. In writing a book such as this, one can only start with an idea. Not to recognize those who brought that idea to fruition is like a concert violinist finishing a particularly moving and difficult piece and then taking bows to the applause of his audience without giving any thought to the importance of his violin in the performance.

When putting together a book of enumerated facts, one can never list all who have made such a book possible, because the required information came from so many sources and people. It is therefore difficult for me to show my appreciation to all those who made this offering possible. To those whom I inadvertently omit, I can only apologize!

There are some people and sources to whom I am forever and irretrievable indebted for the end result of this collection. First, I must tender my appreciation to my mother, Flossie Julia Knowles Cannon, who was born in Texas and enjoyed 92 years of living in the glow of its ever-changing history. She shared so many of her remembrances with me as I grew up, fascinating me with stories told to her when she was just a youngster herself—stories of how the Comanche Indians affected the lives of her ancestors and their neighbors on the Colorado River in Mills County and nearby San Saba River where she grew up. She told me how, when she was young, one could walk through freshly plowed fields after a rain and find arrowheads, and how panthers (probably cougars) from Mexico prowled the mountains near her homeplace. She shared with me many other stories as well, vividly recalled as though they were yesterday. It was during one such session that I learned about "Old Rip" the horned frog of Eastland County fame. And what cops-and-robbers-age boy wouldn't be captivated by stories about Clyde Barrow and Bonnie Parker's exploits told by someone with a first-hand memory of the gangsters' crime sprees? It was always apparent that my mother had just as much curiosity as I do. She was a newspaper clipping fanatic—if it was unusual or bordered on the "believe it or not" category, Mother clipped and saved it. I consider her clipping collection and the many stories she told a real legacy.

I want to express my thanks to Mildred Juniger, my high school journalism teacher who kindled my desire to write, and who grounded me in the basics of journalism. She also provided my first opportunity of writing for publication in our school newspaper, the *Woodrow Wilson News*.

I am thankful to *Texas Highways Magazine* for those items on some of its pages which piqued my interest enough to research them in detail. I could not have assembled this collection without the untiring, beyond-the-call-of-duty assistance of numerous librarians at the Dallas and Irving public libraries, who helped me verify facts from volumes pertaining to Texas history.

It would be gross negligence to omit my wife, Marianne, whose patience must be made of Texas granite, yet softened by bluebonnets. My words of gratitude are not sufficient enough for her tolerance while I took hours out of our days and weeks to write this offering.

To all of these people and sources, I can only say "Thank you!" I am deeply indebted to the *Handbook of Texas* from the Texas State Historical Association, upon which I leaned heavily and often for verification of many trivia items included in this collection. And I would be remiss if I didn't express my appreciation to the 1992-93 *Texas Almanac* for all the assistance it has provided in verifying trivia items and for the additional items I have found and included from its pages. Once again, all I can say is "Thank you!"

Introduction

Trivia is described in *Webster's New World Dictionary* as "unimportant matters; trivialities."

It seems almost ludicrous to link in print the two words *Texas* and *trivia*, or even to link them in the same breath!

Whether one thinks of Texas simply as a land mass or as the Utopia spoken of by its inhabitants as "having the biggest and best of everything known to man," it is difficult to say anything is "trivial" about it! This is the state that was once a republic, a state whose history almost explodes from the pages of history books, a state which boasts a population whose culture is molded from the hundreds of diverse cultures that settled and developed it and elevated it to the preeminence it enjoys among people all over the world today. The evolution of Texas has produced a wealth of little-known facts that are not only informative but interesting and humorous. The reader is sure to find some which prove the old adage, "Truth is stranger than fiction," but take into consideration these bits of trivia are from the state where people believe that boasting is not bragging if it's true!

Truth Is Stranger Than Fiction

Most of us have heard stories that were touted as true, but their contents were so bizarre that they sounded more like the product of an overactive imagination. On the occasion that we find they are indeed true, we are prone to say, "Truth is stranger than fiction." The history of Texas and its people is full of stories such as these. They are the type of stories that, because of their mystique and drama, pique our interest and start our imaginative juices flowing. These stories are just waiting to be exposed and explored. Here are just a few:

The origin of Texas barbecue is an interesting one, to say the least. "Barbecue" is a corruption of the Spanish word *barbacoa*, which was a Sunday breakfast that dates back to the Spanish *vaquero* (cowboy). During the early days of Texas it was customary for a landowner to slaughter a cow at the end of the week. The landowner generally kept the carcass for himself and donated the head to the vaqueros. The vaqueros dug a pit and layered it with mesquite coals and rocks on the bottom, then wrapped the cow's head in wet burlap and lowered it into the coals. They covered the head with rocks and aromatic leaves or dirt and cactus. It was left to steam overnight and ready for a feast Sunday morning.

The common Texas possum is unaffected by the bite of most poisonous snakes, including the copperhead, rattlesnake, and water moccasin.

Legend says that the clock in the county courthouse in Gonzales is cursed. In 1921, though he claimed innocence, Albert Howard was executed in Gonzales. It is said that while he waited to be hanged, he watched the clock on the courthouse as it ticked away his last hours. Howard swore that his innocence would be demonstrated by the clock, which would never keep correct time again. Since his hanging, the four faces of the clock have never kept the same time despite attempts to repair it.

In the 1930s Texas had its very own "Loch Ness Monster." The little town of Italy became a tourist mecca as visitors came from all around to get a glimpse of a much-publicized serpent-like creature reportedly spotted by townspeople and inhabiting a nearby creek. Locals even blamed the serpent for the disappearance of several small children! News releases issued daily from coast to coast kept the nation advised on the serpent's latest movements. Records in the public library in Italy reveal that the monster scare was actually a glorified snake story by R. E. Sparkman, a "stringer" (reporter) for the *Dallas Morning News* who lived in the small, sagging town. He had embellished a story about a boa constrictor that had escaped from a traveling circus performing in Italy. Because its size was so much greater than snakes usually found in the area, reported sightings were exaggerated even more so. One sighter who reported seeing the "monster" cross the highway claimed "its eyes shined bright as automobile headlights." The story grew to such proportions that people in England began inquiring about visiting, and the reporter decided it was time to slow things down. He invented another story, hinting that the United States Army was working on a secret project in the area and had built an invisible wall to keep prying eyes away. The "monster" had crawled behind the invisible wall, he claimed, and therefore could no longer be seen. The thrill-seekers eventually stopped coming, and Italy went back to being a sleepy little town, but not before enjoying another brief economic upswing when the same reporter spun another tale of "long-tailed rabbits" in nearby Chambers Creek. After a California rabbit breeder inquired about showing some of the unusual creatures, a few locals hit upon the idea of showing them at the Fort Worth Fat Stock Show. The rabbits were apparently too wary to be trapped, however, so this phenomenon could never be verified.

Drug abuse is not a new problem in Texas. One of the state's earliest drug laws was passed in 1882 in El Paso. Such a law became necessary because of opium abuse by the Chinese laborers brought in to help build the Southern Pacific Railroad.

One famous Texas battle may owe its name to a European saint. The Battle of San Jacinto in which Texas won its independence took place along the banks of the San Jacinto River. The river was discovered on St.

Hyacinth's Day, August 17. St. Hyacinth was known as the Apostle of Poland and died in 1257.

The "Black Bean Death Warrant" is one of Texas' most interesting bits of trivia, although not trivial to those involved. In December of 1842 a party of Texan soldiers on what was known as the Mier Expedition crossed the border seeking supplies from Mexico. Mexicans captured 176 of the soldiers and all were sentenced to be shot. Then the order was changed and it was decided instead that every tenth man would be shot. An earthen pot containing 159 white beans and 17 black beans was presented to the captured soldiers and each was instructed to draw a bean. Those who drew the black beans were to be shot; the black beans were their "death warrant." One man noticed that the black beans seemed to be larger than the white ones and fingered the beans until he found a smaller one and drew it out. It was indeed a white bean, and the lucky soldier survived.

☆

Ranches and cattle brands have always been a fascination to Texans and non-Texans alike. The lore attached to some of the ranches and their brands are frequently reflective of the state's history. Such is the case with the XIT Ranch and its brand. The ranch was established in 1885 as a piece of land totaling 3,050,000 acres given to the Chicago firm that built the state capitol building in Austin. This massive ranch covered all or at least most of ten counties in Texas. The designer of the XIT livestock brand says that the design was chosen because it would be difficult to alter; however, the brand gave rise to the generally accepted ranch name "Ten-In-Texas" (X standing for ten counties, IT for In Texas).

It sounds like a tall tale to say that the Academy Awards statuette, the Oscar, was named for a Texan, but although he was known to a limited few, Oscar's namesake was indeed a Texan. Oscar Pierce had a niece who worked for the Academy of Motion Picture Arts and Sciences in Hollywood. When she saw the gold statue for the first time, she said, according to legend, "Why, it looks like my Uncle Oscar!"

Many settlers saw Texas as a land of "greener pastures," a real opportunity. Some of them were in such a hurry to get here that they took little time to notify family and friends as to where they had gone. Some simply put up signs that said "GTT," which meant "Gone to Texas." The land, however, attracted its share of those outside the law. The expression "GTT" came into use when Texas developed the reputation of harboring outlaws who had fled to Texas to seek refuge. Some historians have written that GTT was appended to the names of lawbreakers who skipped out, and in some cases, to new arrivals to Texas who were suspected of leaving home under suspicious circumstances.

The popular state ballad "The Yellow Rose of Texas" isn't just about a flower—it is a tribute to a lovely young girl who did much in her own way to help the Texans win their independence from Mexico. Historical accounts say that the "yellow rose" was Emily Morgan, a young mulatto slave girl whom Santa Anna had captured at the James Morgan household and put to work for himself. Emily had been loyal to the Texans and had been able to pass information to them at San Jacinto. About the time the Battle of San Jacinto started it is said that she had General Santa Anna "occupied" in his tent. This gave the Texans a definite battle advantage and allowed them to capture Santa Anna literally with his pants down! According to Martha Ann Turner's book *The Yellow Rose of Texas, Its Saga and Song,* Texans were already in Santa Anna's camp killing Mexican soldiers when he appeared in his red slippers and underwear. The song refers to Emily's skin color.

☆

One could hardly write about Texas curiosities without mentioning "Old Rip," the horned frog (or toad, as some call it) that was entombed in the cornerstone of the Eastland County Courthouse in 1897 and found alive 31 years later, according to published accounts by witnesses. The frog, named for the legendary sleeper Rip Van Winkle of literary fame, was retrieved in February of 1928 when the courthouse was torn down. The frog was alive, although dormant, and after being held a few minutes he began to respond. An article in the *Dallas Morning News* (April 14, 1985) says that "Old Rip" died of pneumonia following a nationwide tour that included a stop at the White House to see President Calvin Coolidge. The elderly frog was laid to rest in a satin-lined casket and put on display in a glass case in the new Eastland County Courthouse.

☆

The only county in Texas named for a woman is Angelina County. When Spanish friars established their mission, San Francisco de la Tejas, they took in an Indian child whom they named Angelina, which means "little angel." She was baptized and learned to speak Spanish; she later became an interpreter for Spanish explorers. The "little angel" also lends her name to a river and a national forest in Texas.

Football has been a vital part of Texas culture since the game began and, consequently, has generated its share of unique and noteworthy stories. Take the poignant tale of Texas A&M University's legendary "12th man." "Non-Aggies" attending an A&M game for the first time are amazed to see the entire student body stand throughout the entire game, except during half-time, at which time they may sit. This strange tradition is based on an event that took place in January 1922 during the "Dixie Classic," the forerunner of the Cotton Bowl. The game was played at Fair Park in Dallas and pitted A&M against Centre College in a bitter contest. According to Kern Tips' *Football Texas Style*, the A&M squad was suffering; injuries had depleted the team to the point that coach Dana Bible wasn't sure he would have enough players to finish the game. Then the coach remembered seeing former player E. King Gill (whom he had released from football to play basketball) sitting in the stands. Coach Bible had Gill brought down from the stands and suited up on the sidelines so that he would be available to play if needed; Gill thus became the team's 12th man. Though the team went on to enjoy a sweet victory that date, it wasn't nearly as precious as the tradition that had been started for the Aggies. Since that unusual "recruitment," A&M fans stand ready, as a body, to show their willingness to play if needed, to be the "12th man."

Another piece of Texas football lore involves the naming of the University of Texas team's mascot, Bevo, a longhorn steer. The Longhorns have one of their fiercest rivals, the Texas A&M Aggies, to thank for it. Determined not to let UT forget a trouncing of 13-0, a group of Aggies kidnapped the steer and branded him with the score. The embarrassed Longhorns, unable to remove the brand, had a running-iron (used by rustlers to alter existing brands on livestock) made. By connecting the 1 and 3 to form a B, altering the - to make an E, and inserting a V before the 0, the shameful score of 13-0 became the word "BEVO." Justifying that this could be a shortened form of "beeves," which means beef cattle, the Longhorns proudly adopted Bevo as the official name of their mascot.

Not many people would find a connection between Jim Bowie, Alamo hero, and Dracula, befanged king of darkness. But strange as it seems, they do have something in common. In 1897 when English novelist Bram Stoker wrote his horror story about Dracula, the English were very enamored with the wild frontier land called Texas. Stoker so loved the Texas mystique that at the end of his novel he assigned heroic Quincy Morris, portrayed as a Winchester-toting, knife-waving, gallant Texan, the bloody deed of plunging a bowie knife into Dracula's heart, killing the "king of vampires."

Another Jim Bowie tale questions the very loyalty of this fallen hero of the Alamo. Bowie was actually a Mexican citizen when he fought at the Alamo, and he was married to a Mexican, two facts that shed a questionable light on Bowie's loyalty. It should be known, however, that prior to the Battle of the Alamo, when Bowie had settled in San Antonio de Bexar, Mexican law required that only

citizens of Mexico could own land in Texas. As Texas land was something Bowie desperately wanted, he decided to become a citizen of Mexico. He converted to Catholicism, and with the sponsorship of his wife and his friend and business partner, Spanish governor Don Juan Martin Veramendi, Bowie's citizenship was granted on October 5, 1830. (His wife Ursula just happened to be Veramendi's daughter.) Despite his connections, Bowie was hailed as a great leader by Sam Houston. Conversely he was considered a great and exceptional soldier by some Mexicans who fought under Santa Anna.
According to legend, as Mexicans soldiers were gathering the Alamo defenders' bodies for cremation after the great battle was done, one Mexican officer wanted to separate Bowie's body from the rest and bury it, because "Bowie's body should not be buried with the masses."
(Nevertheless his was said to have been burned with the rest of the bodies.)

Who would have thought that Christopher Columbus' accidental discovery of the Americas in 1492 would have a link to the State of Texas 500 years later! But it's a hot one: During his quest to find a shortcut to the spice fields of the East Indies, Columbus discovered chili peppers, including the jalapeno pepper historians say natives of America used for thousands of years to season their food. These piquant peppers were so well-liked by the Old World that they were eventually shipped out to all points of the compass. Today, according to the Texas Department of Agriculture, Texas is the largest domestic producer of the jalapeno pepper.

Believe it or not, the wife of a Comanche Indian chief was given land and a pension by the Texas Legislature. Cynthia Ann Parker, a white child who was captured at age nine by the Comanches during a raid on Fort Parker in 1836, was raised by the Indians and later married Chief Peta Nocona. She bore him three children, one of whom, Quanah Parker, later became chief of the Comanches. Although Cynthia Ann's whereabouts were discovered several times, attempts by the whites to get her back were unsuccessful until 1860 when she was recaptured and brought to live with the whites again. Several times she tried to escape and return to the Comanche tribe she felt love and loyalty for. In 1861 the state legislature granted her a pension and a league of land to be administered by a guardian. Cynthia died at her brother's home in Anderson County, Texas, in 1864.

Reference books and lore alike attribute the origin of the term "red light district" to Texas. It's said to have been coined by railroad men after their practice of hanging signal lanterns by the front doors of local brothels while visiting.

One of the best-known examples of Texas eccentricity is the Field of Cadillacs outside Amarillo. The row of ten different year model Caddies was "planted" hood-first in the ground by city inhabitant Stanley Marsh, according to newspaper accounts, simply to display the change in tail-fin design between 1948 and 1964. Supposedly the cars are architecturally positioned to be at the exact angle of the pyramids.

The "Field of Cadillacs" near Amarillo was created by Stanley Marsh.

Though it is said that the term "to bury the hatchet" (let bygones be bygones) originated with the New England Indians, who sealed a peace treaty by ceremoniously burying an ax, their principal weapon of war, apparently this ceremony was also practiced in Texas. When early settlers and Indians in Spanish missions were terrorized by hostile Indians, efforts to make peace resulted in a treaty with the Apaches. According to historians, a ceremony was held in which the Indians buried a live horse as well as a tomahawk and other implements of war.

The job of surveyor today doesn't seem like such a dangerous occupation. But in the early days of Texas, settlers often hired surveyors to locate their land and stake it out, payment being one third of the total acreage. The risk for this reward was great—Indians recognized surveying equipment as "the thing that stole the land," and when the men with the instruments showed up to take away their hunting land, they attacked whenever possible.

Had the *Hindenburg* been filled with Texas helium, one of the world's most infamous disasters might have been prevented. The gigantic German airship burst into flames on May 6, 1937, as it prepared to moor at the Lakehurst Naval Air Station in New Jersey, killing thirty-five passengers and crew aboard and one crewman on the ground. Until then, over a million miles had been safely logged by airship passengers and a cooperative venture was in the works between the U.S., Europe, and South America by American Zeppelin Transport Inc. to fly two nine-million-cubic-foot, helium-filled, American-built dirigibles across the Atlantic and to South America. But the fiery death of the *Hindenburg*, filled with highly flammable hydrogen gas, ended any plans for further use of airships for public transport. Had helium been used in the *Hindenburg*, it might have been a whole different story, but helium was found in only a handful of places, Amarillo, Texas, being one of them. It was rigidly protected under the Helium Act of 1927, which prevented the sale of this precious natural resource—surplus gas could only be leased to American citizens or corporations. Making the unfeasible even more impossible was the fierce, self-sufficient Nazi German pride. Germany never formally requested helium from the U.S. The captain of the *Hindenburg* himself, Ernst Lehmann, was quoted as having said, "Even if we could get helium from America, we wouldn't ask for it." Lehmann was fatally burned in the crash.

The *Hindenburg* airship disaster at Lakehurst May 6, 1937. Photo courtesy of Marvin Krieger Collection.

In the spring of 1945 the war in Europe was nearing conclusion and more attention was turned to the war in the Pacific, thousands of miles away from the rural Texas farming communities of Woodson in Throckmorton County and Desdemona in Eastland County. Both were

farming and ranching communities, and both had sent
fathers and sons to war. The Japanese had begun
launching balloon bombs with incendiary devices
attached in November of 1944, and on March 23-24,
1945, Woodson and Desdemona were "bombed" by the
Japanese, supposedly in retaliation for Jimmy Doolittle's
raid on Tokyo in 1942. No damage was done, and there
were no injuries. The bombs were discovered by school
children and a ranch hand.

With the cost of living ever increasing, it may seem like
our money isn't worth what it used to be. But strange as
it may seem, there was a time in the early days of Texas
when money was worth only a fraction of what it is
today. Take for instance the price of postage. The official
Post Office Department of the Republic of Texas was
approved by an act of Congress on December 20, 1836.
The first postal rates established in Texas were 6¼ cents
for distances of up to 20 miles, 12½ cents for up to 50
miles, 18¾ cents for up to 100 miles, 25 cents for up to
200 miles, and 37½ cents for distances over 200 miles.
These rates applied to single-page letters: a sheet folded
over with the address on the front, since envelopes did
not come into use until 1845. From the beginning,
strong penalties were initiated to deter mail robbery. The
first offense called for a prison term of not more than ten
years. Anyone foolish enough to be involved in a second
offense was sentenced to death by hanging.

In the mid-1800s, one of the state's most lucrative, not
to mention unusual, cash crops could be found literally
at West Texas residents' feet. The availability of the item
in demand kept a steady stream of wagons going to the

plains and coming back loaded with, of all things, buffalo bones, which lay strewn across the desert, free for the picking. Fertilizer companies found that the sun-bleached bones could be used for a number of things and offered $8 to $10 a ton for them. Many hundreds of pounds of the bones were hauled from the principal supplying cities of Sweetwater, Abilene, Baird, Colorado, and Albany. Noted historian, author, and columnist A.C. Greene, who grew up in West Texas, remembers old-timers talking about buffalo bones stacked in piles longer than a city block in Abilene.

Though it is commonly believed that the town of Langtry, Texas, was named for the English actress Lillie Langtry, this is a piece of romantic lore that can be put to rest. Langtry, in Val Verde County, was established in 1881 when the Texas and New Orleans Railroad survey was made. The town was named for a civil engineer in charge of a group of Chinese railroad construction workers. However, Lillie Langtry allegedly did pay a visit to the town supposedly named for her by the eccentric Judge Roy Bean, but she arrived some ten months late to meet the lawman who purportedly named his saloon, the Jersey Lily, in her honor. The judge died in March 1893.

While setting the record straight, we can correct one other piece of misunderstood information which, while not as romantic as the Jersey Lily legend, certainly carries intrigue: the circumstances surrounding the death of one of Texas' most noted benefactors, William Marsh Rice, whose estate was used to establish Rice Institute (now Rice University) in Houston. Rice died in New York at age 85 of what were supposedly natural causes, but investigation revealed that he was murdered by his valet, Charles F. Jones, and an attorney, Albert Patrick, who was allegedly interested in Mr. Rice's estate. While it is doubtful many students at Rice know this story, it's even less known that Mr. Rice's ashes are buried under the statue of him on the Rice campus.

POISON DOSES FOR MILLIONAIRE RICE BEFORE HE DIED.

WORD JUGGLING BY VALET JONES AS HIS MASTER LAY DEAD.

Rice is sinking.—Valet Jones to Dr. Curry.
Rice must have been dead when Jones called me.—Dr. Curry.
Rice is dead.—Valet Jones to the banker.
Rice had been dead for hours.—Fact from death certificate.

DAVID C. SHORT.

MORRIS MEYERS.

| FRAUD, FORGERY, FALSEHOOD. | OVER THE MILLIONAIRE'S CORPSE. |

"Santa Claus wounded in Texas gun battle." Sounds like a tabloid headline, but it's actually true. In an act totally lacking in Yuletide spirit, four bandits, their leader dressed as Santa Claus, entered First National Bank of Cisco on Christmas Eve, 1927, and made off with $12,000. According to newspaper reports, children even followed "Santa" as he went into the bank. But a shoot-out occurred after police were alerted to the robbery and several people, including "Santa," were wounded. The not-so-jolly old elf was captured several days later after a gun battle in South Bend, Texas. Marshall Ratliff ("Santa") was the first of the four robbers to be tried for the crime and was sentenced to die in the electric chair at the state prison in Hunstville. Ratliff was returned to the Eastland County jail on a bench warrant, and in an escape attempt he killed a peace officer, Tom A. "Uncle Tom" Jones, who was helping as a jailer. An angry mob stormed the jail, seized Ratliff, and lynched him.

The story of Chapita (some say Chepita) Rodriguez, the only woman ever legally hanged in Texas, is a mix of fact and legends of the Rio Grande Valley. The name Chapita is a diminutive form of Chepa, the nickname for Josefa. Chapita lived in a hut on the Welder ranch lands on the Arkansas River. San Patricio County records show that in August of 1863 Chapita and Juan Silvera were indicted for murdering a horse trader named John Savage. His body was found in the Arkansas River near Chapita's cabin. When the court met at the town of San Patricio, then the county seat, Juan Silvera was convicted of second-degree murder and given a five-year prison sentence. Chapita was found guilty of first-degree murder and sentenced to be hanged by Judge Benjamin Neal. Mercy was recommended because her conviction was based largely on circumstantial evidence. Nevertheless Judge Neal ordered the sentence to be carried out, and on November 13, 1863, Chapita was hanged from a mesquite tree in the Nueces River bottoms near San Patricio and buried in an unmarked grave. It was later rumored that Chapita's long-lost son was the one who murdered Savage. Another story is that a dying man confessed to the murder. Whatever the truth might have been, Chapita's guilt remains questionable. Legend has it that Chapita's ghost roams the riverbanks where she was hanged. Some even believe there is a curse on the village of San Patricio that brought about its decline—it lost its position as county seat to Sinton in 1893.

☆

Seven flags over Texas? For a short time, there was indeed a seventh flag—that of the "Republican Army of the North." In a plan to free Texas from Spanish rule, Jose Bernado Gutierrez De Lar in 1812 initiated a filibustering expedition in Nachitoches, Louisiana. With the help of U.S. agents, including West Point graduate Augustus William Magee, who was military commander of the Republican Army of the North, a band of rebels and mercenaries crossed the Sabine River into Texas in August and took Nacogdoches. By November La Bahia at Goliad had fallen to them as well. About 800 filibusters defeated 1,200 royalist troops in the Battle of Rosalis; Gov. Manuel de Salcedo surrendered San Antonio on April 1, 1813. Raising the green flag of the Republican Army of the North—sometimes called the "seventh flag over Texas"—Gutierrez and his followers declared the state the "First Republic of Texas." After Gutierrez permitted the execution of fourteen Spanish officers, however, a disgusted Samuel Kemper, who replaced Magee after his death in February 1813, led more than 100 troops back to Louisiana. Gutierrez, undaunted, set up a provisional government. Royalist Col. Elizondo besieged San Antonio with about 990 men, and although Gutierrez's troops defeated the Royalists, their growing hostility toward Gutierrez forced him to return to Louisiana. His remaining troops were ambushed and defeated in the Battle of Medina River south of San Antonio.

The much heralded "Texas hospitality" is evidently taken quite seriously by our celestial neighbors, who interpret literally the phrase "Do drop in anytime." Texas leads all other states and accounts for six percent of the world's known meteor strikes, with 80 cataloged so far. The third-largest meteor crater in the United States is 10 miles southwest of Odessa in Ector County. About 500 feet in diameter and 103 feet deep originally, it has filled in and is only about 5-6 feet deep now. Although fragments have been found and analyzed, the main meteor mass has never been discovered.

According to Big Thicket lore, J.F. Cotton's hogs should be given credit for rooting up more than just acorns. Saratoga, Texas, is credited with having the second oil strike in the Big Thicket. Following the big discovery of oil at Sour Lake, residents of the Big Thicket were conscious of this newly developing resource around them. When Fletcher Cotton noticed his hogs coming out of an area of the thicket slick with a glossy substance, he followed them and discovered the same tell-tale signs that had existed at Sour Lake before oil was discovered. Sour Lake had been a health spa known for its medicinal springs. Neighboring Saratoga Springs took its name from the famous New York spa. Sour Lake continued as a health resort until oil was discovered in 1901. The first producing well in Saratoga in 1903 was brought in two years after the famous gusher Spindletop. Mr. Cotton's hogs really "brought home the bacon."

Texas can accommodate the most ardent of hunters of strange phenomena with not one but two mysterious, unexplainable occurrences: the ghostly Marfa lights (see next entry) and the lesser known "ghost light" of Bragg Road in the already eerie Big Thicket. *Webster's Dictionary* tells us that *supernatural* means "existing outside the normal experience or the known laws of nature." Bragg Road, with its mysterious light, is off Farm-to-Market

Road 1293 and goes through the Big Thicket from the area known as Honey Island to Saratoga. The mysterious ghost light has been reported as "going down the road as though it were someone carrying a flashlight. It has been sighted periodically for over 50 years and is said to manifest itself in many ways. One local reported that he was coming up the "ghost road" one night in a wagon when the light came toward him, continuing on between his team and causing the horses to bolt and break away. The light has been described variously as standing still, floating, and moving quickly, and has been seen in different colors. A few scientific explanations have been offered, including "swamp gas." Local lore blames more exotic and supernatural sources, such as ghosts of murdered railroad workers and spirits of victims lost forever in the thicket. For decades it was thought that the light was a bad omen predicting the end of the world. But whatever the cause of the mysterious illuminations, they are destined to be embellished as the story is retold!

The ghostly phenomenon of the Marfa lights is one known far and wide. These eerie occurrences seem to have an even older history than the Bragg Road lights. In 1883, while moving sheep between Marfa and Alpine in Presidio County, a couple saw a strange light appearing on a mesa near the Chinati Mountains. In the years since, numerous sightings have drawn national attention. The phenomenon is so well known that the 1992-93 *Texas Almanac* lists Marfa as the "city of lights." Some say the lights move; others say they are still, and reports vary as to their color and number. To date there is no proven scientific explanation.

It seems unbelievable that part of Texas would be declared "neutral" to prevent war, but at one time that was the case. After the Louisiana Purchase, the United States and Spain were unable to agree on the boundary between Louisiana and Texas. In order to prevent armed clashes, in November of 1806 an agreement was entered into between the American and Spanish military commanders declaring the disputed territory neutral ground. This neutral area was bound by Arroyo Hondo on the east and the Sabine River on the west. Ownership of the strip eventually went to the United States in the Adams-Onis Treaty of 1821.

Texas has at least one town that was incorporated solely for the purpose of selling liquor. The state of Texas allows some areas to elect whether or not to prohibit the sale of alcohol, and these areas are known as "wet" or "dry" depending on which option they vote for. In 1960 the town of Impact was incorporated just outside of Abilene in Taylor County. Named for Mayor Dallas Perkins' advertising business, the town covered forty-seven square miles and was best known for being the only wet town in dry Taylor County. When two liquor stores opened, a

couple of Abilene lawyers went to court to oppose the town's incorporation. In 1963 the Texas Supreme Court upheld the incorporation and the sale of liquor. The town flourished for sixteen years, building streets and making improvements, but eventually "dried up" after Abilene was voted wet in 1976 and Impact was no longer the closest place to buy alcoholic beverages.

Maria de Jesus de Agreda had a mysterious gift, it's said. Legend has it that she made many an extraordinary pilgrimage to Texas to spread the word of God, all without leaving her native Spain. Maria, who was born in Castile in 1602, grew up in her parents' self-imposed convent, where she gave herself completely to religious contemplation. At age 18 she began to have spells during which her body would become lifeless and she felt herself being transported in her dreamlike state to an unknown land, where she taught religion to "strange and wild people." In 1631, when Father Alonzo de Benavides, who had spent ten years working among the Indians of Texas and New Mexico, visited Maria in Spain, she told him of her fantastic "out of body" expeditions. Father Alonzo had heard this before: between 1621 and 1629 the Jumano Indians of West Texas had told him of a "woman in blue" who had visited them and taught them about the Catholic faith. He concluded that Maria must be this mysterious teacher. She was said to have made as many as 500 visits, in spirit, to Texas between 1620 and 1629 and the legend of her transatlantic pilgrimages was so widely known that King Phillip IV visited her several times.

☆

A sticky subject to touch on is the Texas cactus. Some 100 species of the prickly plant are found in Texas, the widest assortment found in any single state in the United States. They range from the common prickly pear cactus to a rare variety found only in El Paso. Texas also grows cacti of radically different sizes, from the button cactus, which is no larger than a dime, to the barrel cactus, also known as the fishhook cactus, which can weigh in at half a ton. As formidable as their protective spines may seem, however, with proper preparation many cacti can be eaten by humans and livestock. Texas cacti have an interesting array of names as well, from pleasant to amusing to painful-sounding! These include hunger, starvation, flapjack, dumpling, strawberry, blind pear,

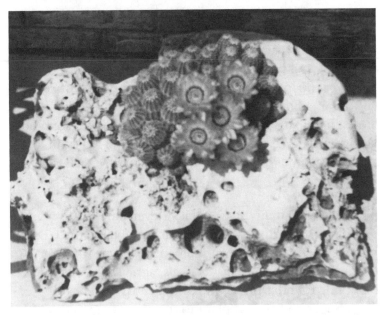

This Texas rainbow cactus growing from a small pocket of soil shows how little nourishment is required to produce a healthy cactus. This accounts, no doubt, for the prolific cactus population in Texas. Much of which is arid, rocky soil!

cow's tongue, night blooming cactus, devil's head, horse-killer, rainbow, pin cushion, porcupine, lady-finger, and "Glory of Texas" (which, oddly enough, grows mainly in Mexico!).

Have you ever heard of a town being ruled by a walking cane? Back in Texas' infancy, the top city official or mayor was called by the Spanish name for town leader—*alcalde.* As a sign of office, the alcalde carried a silver-headed cane, and when he couldn't appear in person, he could be represented by sending his cane!

Clay Allison, renowned Texas rancher and gunfighter, was known as "Clay Allison of the Washita." In the 1870s he appeared in Colfax County, New Mexico, allegedly after fighting an unusual duel in a roomy grave dug by his opponent and him. The winner was supposed to shovel dirt over the loser. Allison did the shoveling. Maurice Fulton, in a book about Allison, writes that after a life of lead-slinging against such notables as Bat Masterson and Wyatt Earp, Allison met his death when he fell from a loaded wagon and was crushed beneath its wheels.

Although they may not know it or even care, many convicted felons in Southeast Texas can blame the Civil War for their places of confinement and type of labor. According to the *Handbook of Texas,* agriculture was the economic foundation of Brazoria County in its early days. Sugar and cotton plantations along the rivers and deeper creeks flourished during the antebellum period in Texas, making Brazoria the wealthiest county in the state. With abolition and the freeing of slaves, however, agriculture declined sharply in this region, and many of the plantations were broken into small farms and turned into pasture land. Other land parcels became the Ramsey, Clemens, and Darrington prison farms of the Texas Department of Corrections. Agricultural efforts on this land still exist but are now performed not under the watchful eye of the master's overseer but instead under the eye of an armed guard whose job is to help the laborer learn that "crime doesn't pay."

There was a time when Mexico meant the difference in Texans having or not having that special cake or pie! We depended on our neighbors to the south for the sugar that enabled us to make that Sunday treat. In the 1940s when World War II brought about the rationing of sugar, Texans along the Rio Grande River trekked across the bridges into Mexico to bring back supplies of the coveted sweetener.

For nearly 200 years the name Waterloo has been synonymous with defeat and doom. Even *Webster's New World Dictionary* defines Waterloo as a "town in Belgium, scene of Napoleon's final defeat (1815); any disastrous or decisive defeat." Was it just a matter of geography or a cynical, political predestination that Austin, the Texas state capital, was originally named Waterloo? According to the *Texas Almanac*, "In 1839 the Texas Congress authorized a commission to select a permanent capital. It was to be north of the Old San Antonio Road between the Trinity and Colorado Rivers. It was to lie on major north-south, east-west trade routes and near the center of the state. The commission selected a site near Waterloo, an outpost on the Colorado River, about eighty miles north of San Antonio. The location was enhanced by its mild climate and plentiful water from nearby springs. In building the city, the town lots were sold in 1839 at a total income of $182,585, which practically paid for the government buildings under construction."

In his writings about growing up in the Howard County town of Coahoma in the 1930s, Hub Hagler tells of the activities seen on Highway 80, which was the main connecting highway between New York and Los Angeles. Hub writes that in 1932 two men bet on the governor's race. The loser had to pull the winner along the stretch of Highway 80 that ran from Fort Worth to El Paso in a child's coaster wagon. The man doing the pulling had a heavy leather belt around his waist attached to the wagon tongue. The rider sat in a chair in the wagon. This all transpired during the Great Depression, which caused some people to do some strange things.

Hub also writes about the "Bunion Derby" which was a foot race run from Los Angeles to New York City in 1928. The race, promoted by C.C. Pyle, promised a cash prize of $25,000 to the first-place winner. Some 275 men and women started the race, but by the time they reached Coahoma the number was down to 75. The *Historical Sports Almanac* reports that "55 runners finished the race at Madison Square Gardens with only 19 people waiting to witness the finish of the race." Andrew Payne won and claimed the cash prize. The promoter claimed he lost $150,000 on the event.

In this story he writes about how the Texas "dress code" has changed over the years. In 1932 a California family traveling through Big Spring stopped at a service station and the man of the family got out wearing shorts. A nearby policeman spotted him with his legs exposed and ordered the tourist to get out of town or dress himself properly before venturing into public!

Incidentally, Big Spring derives its name from the "big spring" in Sulphur Draw which was a watering place for buffalo, coyote, lobo, and wild mustang. Contrary to popular lore, there is no evidence that the town was originally named Big Springs and dropped the "s" when one of the springs dried up. Signal Mountain, ten miles southeast of Big Spring, was a topographical landmark for early cattlemen.

At one time the entire Texas navy was rented to another country! In 1841 Mirabeau B. Lamar, president of the Republic of Texas, made an alliance with Yucatan, which was then in revolt, to rent out the Texas navy (all three ships) for $8,000 a month. When Sam Houston was inaugurated, he promptly ordered the fleet back to Texas. Since the Yucatans didn't expect the Mexicans to fight for eight months or a year, they suspended the agreement with the understanding that it could be renewed when the Texas navy was needed again.

Gringo, the Latin American slang word used to denote English-speaking foreigners, especially North Americans, originated during the Mexican-American War of 1846-1848. A popular soldier's song sung by Americans contained the phrase "Green grow the violets," which to the Mexicans who heard it sounded like "gringo" instead of "green grow." The term was thereafter associated with the "Norte Americanos."

A river higher than its banks? The Rio Grande River actually flows through the Rio Grande Valley at a higher elevation than its surrounding terrain. Over many years the river has flooded many times, leaving rich sand deposits and creating a natural levee.

What's in a name? Perhaps nothing if your life revolves around the same name, as is the case in this piece of South Texas trivia:

Santa Gertrudis cattle, a distinctively Texas breed, were developed on the gigantic King Ranch in Texas by Robert Justice Kleberg. The breed was named for the Santa Gertrudis land grant from which the ranch was built. The King Ranch had its beginning in 1852, when Richard King purchased a Spanish land grant of 75,000 acres in Nueces County on the Santa Gertrudis Creek. After King's death, his widow asked his lawyer—Kleberg—to manage the ranch. It was under Kleburg's management that the now famous breed of cattle was developed. Kleberg married King's daughter, Alice Gertrudis King. Kleburg's ranch, his cattle, and his wife's name originate from the same root.

Though Texas has a legendary reputation for bragging and spectacular stories, the Crash near Crush seems almost too much even for the natives to believe. But on September 15, 1856, George Crush, a passenger agent for Missouri, Kansas & Texas Railroad, engineered the publicity stunt of all time when he carried out his idea of

having two M.K.&T. steam locomotives run at each
other at 90 mph. He was hoping the event would attract
enough passengers on special trains to pay for it. Some
50,000 spectators arrived on thirty special trains and
assembled in a field between West and Waco to see the
great crash, which was catastrophic if not spectacular.
Two people were killed and many injured when the two
boilers exploded. The railroad settled all claims by the
injured as fast as they were presented. As far as is known,
no similar stunt has been tried again.

The town of Cuero in DeWitt County is known as the
"Turkey Capital of the World." The town's name is
actually Spanish for "hides," so named because the
Indians told the Spaniards that the name of a nearby
creek (also Cuero) meant hides. But all that aside, Cuero
got its turkey title when the town initiated the Turkey
Trot in 1912 to herald the opening of the fall market
season. The Turkey Trot was the practice of turkey
buyers to drive flocks of the birds into Cuero after
buying them from outlying farms. Cuero is not the only
Texas town with a fowl reputation; the community of
Turkey was so named because of the wild turkeys found
on nearby Turkey Roost Creek. The original name of the
town was Turkey Roost but it was changed to Cuero
when the post office was established.

Who is buried in Sam Bass's grave? There are some who
believe the legendary outlaw's remains are buried not at
Round Rock but elsewhere in Texas. This theory
maintains that Sam Bass survived the ambush at Round
Rock and managed to make it to the town of Grapevine
in Tarrant County before his wounds did him in.

According to Grapevine mayor Bill Tate, who is well-versed in Bass lore, Bass had family living in Grapevine. Tate remembers as a child going with his father to hoe graves at local cemeteries. At the Old Hall Cemetery in Lewisville in Denton County, he remembers seeing a marker engraved "Sam Bass." Although that could have been for another deceased man of the same name, it nevertheless piqued Tate's interest in the legendary Bass's fate. According to a book published by the Grapevine Historical Society, *Grapevine Area History*, Bass was buried in a cemetery near Grapevine. Billie Sparger, who says Bass was her great-grandfather James A. Hensley's brother-in-law, gives this account in the book: "Several of the gang were killed that day. Sam, himself, was mortally wounded. The sheriff picked up one young man, yelling, 'I shot Sam Bass!'. They hauled the dead man through the town yelling all the way, 'Sam Bass is dead, come see Sam Bass!'. They buried the poor man in the Round Rock Cemetery. Even today people come from all over to see his grave. Sam, though badly wounded, managed to make it to the railroad tracks not far away.... The story goes that when he got to Grapevine, Sam was, indeed, dead. The man at the depot knew James Hensley. He sent a man to tell him to come about Sam. According to Grandpa Hensley, when he got there, the main man at the depot had Sam dressed, wrapped in a blanket, and placed in a pine box. Grandpa paid him and told him 'Keep quiet about this.' Grandpa Hensley did a lot of business there and knew he could trust him. James Hensley and two black men at the ranch, Dad Nelson and another man, placed Sam on a wagon and buried him by lantern light, in a secret place, where he could rest in peace." Elsewhere in the book it is mentioned that "Bass was buried during the night at Parker Memorial Cemetery near the Hensley family plot."

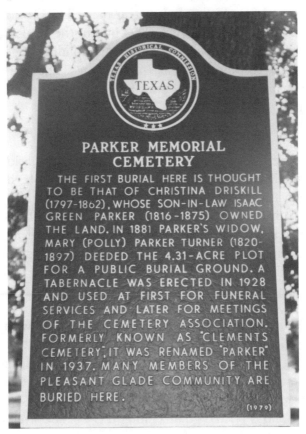

The word *Tejas*, from which comes the word Texas, is said to be the Spanish rendition of the greeting Spanish explorers received from the Hasinai (Caddoan) Indians and means friend or ally.

Although it might seem like an unconventional place for a political convention, one Texas governor was nominated for office in a streetcar barn! The Democratic state convention of August 1892 met in the Houston streetcar barn because it was the only building large enough to accommodate all the delegates. The "car-barn convention" nominated James Hogg, who was re-elected governor that same year.

One little bit of Texas that has influenced our national pastime is the term "Texas-leaguer," which can be heard on televised baseball games. A Texas-leaguer is a fly ball that is hit too far to be snagged by an infielder but too short to be caught by an outfielder. How this term came to be associated with Texas is not known, but ball player Harry Raymond is said to have coined the term in 1888.

The Winchester Quarantine had nothing to do with diseased firearms. It was in fact an "extra-legal device" used by Panhandle ranchers to staunch the northward movement of cattle that might spread the cattle tick. Charles Goodnight of the J.A. Ranch and O.H. Nelson of the Shoe Bar posted guards along the 45-mile stretch between the ranches so that nesters moving north were required to go around the line or turn the cattle over to the watchmen until the first frost. Because of the ready-loaded guns of the guards, the line was called the "Winchester Quarantine."

Think only roller coasters run on wooden rails? Think again. The Rusk Transportation Company was formed in May of 1874 to build a tramway from Rusk to

Jacksonville to connect the International Great Northern Railroad. This link was formed to protect the territory of the people of Rusk. The line was financed locally and funds were scarce, so every effort was made to cut costs. Iron rails were deemed too expensive so the company laid wooden ones. Although the rail line was only a few miles long, sometimes the trip took all day because of problems with the wooden rails.

Marshall, Texas, was at one time the capital of Missouri. How, you ask? Well, after the fall of Vicksburg to Union forces in 1863, the city of Marshall became the civil authority west of the Mississippi River, and as a fortified city it housed the capital of the state of Missouri. It remained the capital until the South capitulated. Governor Thomas C. Reynolds and his staff had their headquarters there.

San Elizario, a town located about twenty miles south of El Paso on the Rio Grande River, was the county seat of El Paso County from 1850 until 1876. Originally the town and its presidio were probably on the Mexican side of the Rio Grande, but because of a change in the river's course in the early nineteenth century, the village ended up on the American bank. United States troops were stationed there in 1850, and the California Column made its headquarters there in 1862. The county seat moved to Ysleta in 1876.

The Stetson hat, icon of Texas style, was actually the creation of Yankee ingenuity. John B. Stetson of Philadelphia, who went West to regain his health in the

1860s, fashioned himself a big hat that would protect him from rain, sun, and wind. After his return to Philadelphia, Stetson made a hat which he called "boss of the plains" and sent it to Western dealers. The Texas Rangers adopted the hat and found it could be used for many things: to drink from, water one's horse, fan a campfire, blindfold a stubborn horse, smother a grass fire, and slap a steer. The hat also could serve as a target in gunfights. Then it could be brushed off for dress wear. Because of its versatility and durability, the hat became a distinguishing characteristic of the cowboy, as well as one of the popular features of Western fiction.

The Texas Highway Department has proof that Texas really is "heaven on earth," as some of our streets are indeed paved with gold, and further proof is stated on a historical marker five miles south of Ringgold on U.S. 81. The pavement on sections of U.S. 81 and U.S. 287 in Montague County contains gold. When the two highways were being paved in 1936, sand for the concrete was taken from a nearby pit. Seeing glints of gold in the sand, the owner of the pit had samples tested, but although the laboratory confirmed that it was gold, there was only about 54 cents' worth of gold per ton of ore, and it was very difficult to separate from the sand, making it not worth the expense. In all, sand containing about $250,000 worth of gold was mixed into the concrete for thirty-nine miles of the two highways.

In his book *Mean as Hell*, the story of his life as a lawman in early Texas, R.D. (Dee) Harkey (a distant cousin of this author) told how his brother Jim Harkey and Jim Barbee killed each other over Harkey's singing "Yankee

Doodle." In 1878 both men were cowhands in the Panhandle, sharing a lineshack on the Pease River, when Harkey chided Barbee over Barbee's saying that he had attempted to kill his father with a butcher knife. According to a freighter to whom Harkey had related the circumstances of the fight before he died, Harkey started singing "Yankee Doodle" and an argument broke out between the two over Harkey singing "that dumb song." The two had further words and Barbee fired his revolver at Harkey. Harkey died later but not before firing four rounds into Barbee, killing him on the spot.

In 1956 the Chrysler Corporation produced an automobile model specially to be sold in Texas. Called the Dodge Texan, its sales brochures boasted, "The name is proudly emblazoned on both rear fenders. And the brave crossed flags of the Lone Star State are right up front where your fellow Texans can admire them." The crossed flags were indeed  prominently displayed on the front of the automobile. This was, unfortunately, in violation of the protocol for use of the Texas flag, which says "Pictures of the flag shall not be used in an advertisement." According to Chrysler representatives, the emblems were used for three months until a complaint was filed by the Daughters of the Republic of Texas. Subsequently the flags were removed.

A saloon-keeper in Granbury, before his death in 1903, made an astonishing admission: he was President Lincoln's assassin, John Wilkes Booth. According to the *Dallas Times Herald* (July 28, 1978), residents believed the claim of John St. Helen, who had moved to Granbury five years earlier and frequently quoted Shakespeare. Booth had been a noted Shakespearean actor. After his death St. Helen's body was mummified and exhibited in traveling circuses. Adding to the mystery, the body reportedly disappeared in 1938.

A number of unwilling Texans allegedly participated in the building of the bridge made famous in the post-WWII book, movie, and song, *Bridge over the River Kwai*. These reluctant Texas workers were members of the 2nd Battalion, 131st Field Artillery of the 36th Infantry Division of the Texas National Guard. Later dubbed "The Lost Battalion" by newspapers, this battalion along with Dutch, Australian, and British forces surrendered to invading Japanese forces on Java. They were taken prisoners of war, and the United States could not or would not disclose what happened to the unit; thus the nickname, "The Lost Battalion." Over the next forty-two months the men were confined to such projects as building roads and railroad construction including building the now-famous bridge over the River Kwai.

Effie Thomas, a 100-year-old resident of the Christian Care Center in Mesquite, told of her pioneer teaching days in the Panhandle near the famous Goodnight Ranch. She related how an area rancher named Cobel had an accredited school built on his ranch and got state aid to hire a teacher, who, incidentally, boarded at the

Cobel home. She taught the school's only pupil, Cobel's daughter, who couldn't attend existing schools because of the distance.

Effie Thomas, on her 100th birthday.

The bois d'arc tree, whose name means "wood of the bow," was named by French explorers moving southward who noticed that the tree was selected for bows by the Indians because of its strength and resiliency. Bois d'arc was also used in making wagons. Victor Doerle was an early Dallas blacksmith who constructed wagons using bois d'arc wood at his shop on Commerce Street between Houston and Record Streets. Bois d'arc also helped lift Dallas out of the mud: According to local historians, the wood, cut into blocks, was used to pave Dallas streets in the 1880s. At that time the city accepted no responsibility for street paving, so the cost was borne by residents whose property abutted the street on both sides. The strong trees also served as fences between properties. These durable trees, planted as fences or property markers, are still quite common.

Just when you thought it was safe to be back in the U.S. . . . some eighty-one years after Texas won her independence from Mexico and seventy-two years after Texas became a state, Mexico was given a chance to reclaim it through a bizarre plot hatched in Germany. According to the *World War One Source Book*, Germany's secretary of state, A. Zimmerman, sent a coded cable to Germany's ambassador to Mexico, Von Eckhardt, on January 19, 1917, which contained an unusual proposal: In the event of hostilities between Germany and the United States, Germany should assist Mexico in recapturing their lost territories of Texas, New Mexico, and Arizona, and Japan should be invited into the Mexican-German alliance. British Naval Intelligence intercepted and decoded the cable and passed it to Walter Page, U.S. Ambassador to Britain, and Page forwarded it to the U.S. State Department. President Wilson published the note on March 1, 1917. This caused widespread indignation in the U.S., and although Mexico and Japan denied it, this event, along with other German intrigue, had a considerable effect on political and public opinion and paved the way for a U.S. declaration of war on Germany on April 16, 1917.

Though Texas is thought of by many as flat and prairie-like (and some parts indeed are), at one time Texas had some great ski slopes. An 1836 map shows that the Republic of Texas included that portion of

Colorado in which is located one of today's most popular ski resorts, Crested Butte.

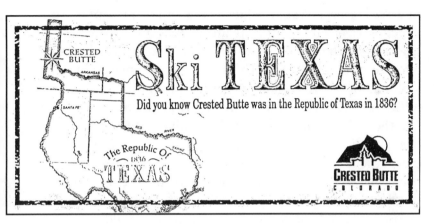

"The Eyes of Texas," the official song of the University of Texas and accepted by most as the unofficial state song of Texas, was originally written as a prank! According to the *Handbook of Texas*, the Glee Club at UT serenaded school president William L. Prather at a varsity minstrel show in 1903 with lyrics written by John Lang Sinclair sung to the tune of "I've Been Working on the Levee." The words were a take-off of the president's frequent admonition to students, "The eyes of Texas are upon you!" The song became popular with the entire student body and was adopted as the official song of UT. It took on a more serious tone when students were asked to sing it at Prather's funeral in 1905.

Many interesting Texas tales involve the San Bernard River. One of the most fascinating is the mysterious wailing violin sound which has earned the waterway the nickname of "the singing river." Some blame the musical sounds on escaping gas. Nola McKey of Austin, writing in *Texas Highways Magazine*, relates the following stories which have attempted to explain the mournful tones heard along the river's lower reaches: "One story tells of a former pirate from Jean Lafitte's band who played his violin along the riverbanks. After the pirate was murdered, his ghost began playing the plaintive music. Another tale claims that a longboat full of slaves overturned at the San Bernard's mouth. Chained in place, the slaves could not escape, and all drowned. To some, the river's haunting sound represents the wails of the dying. Yet another legend tells of a young musician whose bride-to-be died just hours before the wedding. The grief-stricken lover played his violin nightly, trying to console himself. Ever since his death, his sad song has continued."

Even though John Neely Bryan founded Dallas, there was a time, according to his own letters, when he did not feel welcome in the city. The Dallas Historical Society as well as several books provide information that indicate that at his death Bryan was buried in a pauper's graveyard. The legends of Bryan's decline claim that he left Dallas in 1849 to join the gold rush in California. It is said that Bryan was totally unsuccessful in finding his fortune and fell on hard times, becoming an alcoholic. His writings indicate that when he left Dallas he left behind some enemies and generally destroyed his physical and mental health. Although it is not confirmed, it is believed that Bryan ended up in the state mental asylum where he died September 14, 1877, and was buried in a pauper's plot in Austin, many miles away from the city he founded.

One of the most sought-after holiday foods at Christmastime in Texas is the shuck-wrapped hot tamale. According to the Mexican Consulate, the spicy meat-and-masa staple found on most Tex-Mex menus is a traditional Christmas food in the Hispanic culture. Nola McKey writes in *Texas Highways Magazine* that " . . . traditionally people had to wait until the first frost, when the weather was cooler, to start the hog-butchering process. This meant tamales were made during the winter months, close to the holidays."

The towns of Jonesborough (now Jonesboro) and Pecan Point shared the distinction of being the first Anglo-American settlements in Texas. Jonesborough was located in what is now Red River County and was actually the county seat of an Arkansas county. According to the *Handbook of Texas*, "the expulsion of settlers north of the Red River by United States troops increased the population of Jonesborough prairie after 1821, and the number was further augmented by the dissolution of Miller County, Arkansas Territory, in 1925. In 1832 Jonesborough was chosen the county seat of Miller County, which was situated wholly on the south side of the Red River after 1828."

There is no longer any written documentation, but a descendent of one of the parties involved tells of a huge blunder in the design of the elegant Galvez Hotel on Galveston Island, long a playground for socialites, politicos, and others of society's "upper crust." In all its grandeur, the Galvez was designed with no provisions for a kitchen. Those connected with its construction claim that after bids had been let, it was discovered that the plans did not include a kitchen, so one was built in a separate building to "cover up" the error. The hotel where band leader Phil Harris and Alice Fay were married and where President Franklin D. Roosevelt stayed when he went deep-sea fishing in the Gulf nevertheless did much to breathe life into a sagging island economy, attached kitchen or no.

Lost in the Footnotes of Texas History

There are countless intriguing facts about Texas and Texans that are virtually unknown because they have fallen through the cracks of historical remembrance. They are like footnotes that have, somehow, slipped off the bottom of the pages of Texas history, never to see the light of day until they are ferreted out and then relegated to what we call "trivia." A few of these facts have found their way into this volume.

Although the patent eluded him, a well-to-do cattleman and inventor from West Texas, D.G. Gilbreath, who moved to Mineral Wells and built the Hexagon Hotel, by lore is reputed to have invented a well-known item used in most offices around the world today. The item? The paper clip.

The last public hanging in Texas took place on July 30, 1923, in Waco when Roy Mitchell was executed for one of eight murders he committed during a reign of terror.

☆

The reason there is no period after the Dr in Dr Pepper is, according to a company official, that it was dropped in the 1930s because the period designates the name as that of a medical doctor, which, of course, the soft drink is not!

Dr Pepper's 10, 2 and 4 regimen was emphasized on the highly visible clock tower atop the company's former headquarters on Mockingbird Lane in Dallas. The building was completed in 1948. It remained the firm's headquarters until August, 1988. The 26 acres on which it sits was originally a part of the old Caruth family farm.

☆

America's most purchased and favorite food, the hamburger, was invented by a Texan. The hamburger got its start in the Henderson County town of Athens in the 1880s. Fletcher Davis served up a meat patty topped with mustard, a pickle, and onions, between two slices of bread. The sandwich caught on, and Davis introduced the hamburger at the World's Fair in St. Louis in 1904.

For many years, thousands of visitors to Houston have lodged themselves at the Rice Hotel without realizing it was once the capital of the Republic of Texas. Before Houston was fully developed, the Allen Brothers offered to, at their own expense, build a building to be used by the government if their city was selected as the republic's capital. They proceeded to build a frame, two-story building for the first capitol. This building, which was on the site of the present-day Rice Hotel, served as capitol from 1837 to 1839.

John Bell Hood was commander of the Confederate troops in Texas during the Civil War.

One famous landmark in Texas was named for the cottonwood tree. The Spanish mission Alamo was named for a grove of cottonwood trees nearby; *alamo* is the Spanish word for cottonwood.

The colors in the Texas flag have a special significance: red for courage, white for liberty, and blue for loyalty.

One of Texas' most celebrated holidays is known by a nickname. June 19 is the date in 1865 when Union General Granger announced, for the first time, the emancipation of Texas slaves. Texas blacks celebrate this day as "Juneteenth."

☆

Legend has it that in the Battle of San Jacinto, in which
Texas won her independence from Mexico, many
Mexican soldiers were heard making the plaintive cry,
"Me no Alamo! Me no Goliad!" The suppliants made
these pleas in hopes of receiving mercy from the Texans
by disavowing involvement in the two best-known
massacres of Texans. At the Alamo many Texans died
because of Santa Anna's orders to "show no mercy." And
on March 27, 1836, Col. James Fannin and 352 of his
soldiers were executed though they were prisoners of war
held at La Mission La Bahia at Goliad. Subsequently the
Texans' battle cry became "Remember the Alamo,
remember Goliad." Keenly aware of the atrocities they
had committed, the Mexicans knew the wrath of the
Texans and sought every way possible not to become
victims of it.

☆

Much has been said about the legendary Bowie knife,
but there is enough material on the subject to conclude
that the knife was not made by the Alamo hero. While
recovering from the "Sand Bar duel" in Natchez,
Mississippi, Jim Bowie was given the knife by his brother,
Rezin Bowie. The details of the making of the knife,
which became the hand weapon of choice for many in
the Southwest before the advent of the six-shooter, are
not fully known. One widely told story, which is said to
originate from a Bowie relative, is that Rezin had the
knife made to his specifications, which included a large
guard between the handle and the blade to prevent the
user's fingers from being cut should they slip over the
blade during use. It is said that the knife was made in

Ayoyelles Parish, Louisiana, from a file in Rezin's blacksmith shop by his blacksmith, Jesse Cliffe.

Many visitors to Waxahachie admire its county courthouse without realizing that in its stonework are unflattering carvings of a former resident! The building is famous locally for its curious connection to a spurned love affair. An Italian stone carver employed to sculpt the courthouse's stone columns boarded with the Frame family. He fell in love with the daughter, Mabel, and in an act of amour chiseled her image in the courthouse facade. Unfortunately, Mabel did not return his affections. The rejected suitor continued to carve her likeness in the stone, making it progressively uglier!

The Ellis County Courthouse in Waxahachie, Texas.

☆

The rock 'n' roll magazine *Rolling Stone* is a not a new
name to Texans—a magazine named *Rolling Stone* was
published in Austin, Texas, between 1894 and 1895. It
contained humorous articles, political notes, cartoons,
and jokes and was published by Sydney Porter, who came
to Texas from North Carolina. Porter went on to bigger
fame writing under the pseudonym of O. Henry but was
later charged with embezzlement from a bank where he
had worked as a teller. He fled to Central America; in
1897 he returned from Honduras to visit his sick wife
and was arrested in March 1898. He was found guilty
and sentenced to the federal penitentiary in Columbus,
Ohio. It was there that Porter began writing short stories,
many of which had Texas settings.

☆

A one-time powerful Texas politico tried to make his
favorite flower, the cactus flower, the Texas state flower.
The Colonial Dames of Texas spoke for the bluebonnet,
including presenting an oil painting of that flower to the
legislators, many of whom had never seen the flower, and
got the bluebonnet designated as the state flower. John
Nance (Cactus Jack) Garner, then vice president, lost his
bid for the cactus.

☆

One of our best-loved Christmas symbols is named for a
transplanted Texan. The poinsettia is named for Joel
Poinsett, an amateur botanist originally from South
Carolina. It's said that while Poinsett served as the first
United States minister to Mexico from 1825 to 1829, he
took a liking to the showy flower while living in Texas.

When he introduced the flower to Washington, it was named after him.

Imagine there being five states of Texas! According to the book *Annexation of Texas*, published in 1919, the resolution adopted by Congress allowing the annexation of Texas had the provision that Texas could be divided into states of convenient size not to exceed four, in addition to the said state of Texas. Add them up: five states! And each would doubtless want a part of the Alamo!

Sam Houston, Texas' first president and the first governor, was given the name "the Raven" by the Cherokee Indians when he lived with them in Tennessee. The chief of the band selected the name because of the "powerful medicine" of the bird in Cherokee mythology.

Johanna Troutman is given official credit for designing the "Lone Star" flag of Texas, although there were several flags bearing the lone star used in various Texas battles. Mrs. Troutman, however, is referred to as the Betsy Ross of Texas. The Lone Star flag was approved in 1839.

In the 1800s Texas ranchers used four major cattle trails to drive their cattle to railheads so they could be shipped to market. They were the Shawnee Trail, the Chisolm Trail, the Western Trail, and the Goodnight-Loving Trail. Hundreds of thousands of longhorn cattle were driven up these trails to be shipped to markets across the United States.

When honorary General Walter Williams died in 1959 at the age of 117, one of America's most important periods of history came to an end. Williams was the last surviving soldier of the Civil War, having served in Hood's Texas Brigade during the final months of the war. When the last surviving Union soldier died in 1956, Dwight Eisenhower bestowed upon Williams the honorary rank of general. He was buried in a Confederate general's uniform.

☆

The last hostile Indian attack on whites in Texas occurred in 1874 at Adobe Walls in Hutchinson County. The raid was instigated by a war-mongering medicine man and led by Comanche Chief Quanah Parker, who assembled a war party and attacked the buffalo camp. Chief Parker, the last Comanche Indian chief, was the son of an Indian father and a white mother, Cynthia Ann Parker, who was captured as a small girl at Fort Parker, Texas. Some contend that the last hostile action with Indians in Texas was after 1874 when General Ranald S. Mackenzie defeated a large force of Indians at Palo Duro Canyon, one of the last Indian strongholds in the state, in order for Anglo-Americans to make a permanent settlement in the area.

☆

That San Antonio was settled by immigrants from a group of islands in the Atlantic seems so unreal that the fact is almost forgotten by most Texans. On June 13, 1772, the Marquis San Migual de Aguayo sent a report to the King suggesting that two hundred settlers be brought to San Antonio from Cuba or the Canary

Islands. The Spanish crown took Aguayo's advice, but bureaucracy moves slowly and it was not until 1731 that fifteen families—fifty-six people—arrived in San Antonio. The group joined the missionaries, soldiers, and ranchers to form the first self-government. Called the Villa of San Fernando de Bexar, the settlement was named in honor of the King's son.

A Dutchman of "questionable honesty" is the namesake for Bastrop County and was influential in obtaining land grants to attract some of the first Anglo settlers to Texas. Some believe that Baron de Bastrop, who was born in Holland, was a tax collector there and absconded with all the tax revenues. But here, Bastrop seems to have done good. He used all his influence with the Spanish governor of Texas to get him to listen to Moses Austin, father of Stephen F. Austin. Moses had approached the governor with plans to bring Anglo colonists to settle Texas, but the plan had been rejected and Austin was told to leave. De Bastrop was very influential with the governor and intervened for Austin. As a result, Austin was able to get land grants and to bring 300 families into Texas. These first families went on to be known in history as "the old 300."

To many who have studied Texas history, the term "a league and a labor" has managed to slip from our recollection. We were taught that this term was a Spanish land measurement and was the amount of land granted to the heads of the households of the first Anglo settlers. A labor was a Spanish land unit measuring 177 acres. Under the Mexican Colonization Act by which the first settlers entered the Stephen F. Austin colony in

Texas, heads of families engaged in farming received a labor of land. Cattle raisers received a *sitio* or league (4,428 acres). Most settlers combined ranching and farming and got a league and a labor.

Sam Houston's record of public service is long, all the more impressive since it was accomplished with a minimum education. An abbreviated view of his life reveals that in 1818 he began studying law on his own in Nashville, Tennessee. After a few months he opened a law office in Lebanon, Tennessee, and that same year was elected district attorney for the Nashville district. He was appointed adjutant general with the rank of colonel, and in 1821 he was elected to the rank of major general. Houston was seated in the United States Congress without opposition in 1823 and re-elected in 1825. Two years later he became governor of Tennessee, and in 1829 Houston was granted citizenship into the Cherokee Nation and served as Indian Agent to the U.S. in Washington. In 1835, after moving to Texas, Houston was elected major general in the Texas army. He was a signer of the Texas declaration of independence from Mexico and commander-in-chief of the Texas army. In 1836 Houston was elected president of the Republic of Texas and was re-elected in 1841. He also represented Texas in the U.S. Senate for fourteen years. Houston was also governor of Texas. Whew! All this was accomplished in spite of the fact that Houston's only formal education was a few terms in neighborhood schools.

Santa Anna's brutality at the Alamo is well known, but historians tell us of at least one act of benevolence on his part after the battle of the Alamo, when the Mexican

General Gave ordered his soldiers to collect the bodies of the defenders to be burned. One of the soldiers, Francisco Esparza, began searching for the body of his brother, Gregorio, who had fought with the defenders. When he found the body, he and his widowed sister-in-law went to Santa Anna and begged permission to give Gregorio a Christian burial. Santa Anna granted permission, and Gregorio Esparza was removed and buried near the San Fernando church, the only Alamo defender accorded such an honor.

The Alamo, in San Antonio, Texas.

Had it not been for Clara Driscoll, we might not have an Alamo today. Born in 1881, Clara was educated in Texas and France. In 1903 she bought the Alamo to keep it from being torn down and funded extensive restoration. This earned her the title, "Savior of the Alamo."

The story of the "come and take it" flag is one that is often overlooked. The town of Gonzales was the westernmost point of Anglo-American civilization in Texas in 1836. Much of the Texas revolutionary activity was centered there, such as the Battle of Gonzales on October 2, 1835. The town was known as "The Lexington of the Texas Revolution," as the first battle of the revolution was fought there. The battle grew out of Mexican demands for a cannon which had been given to the colonists at Gonzales as a defense against the Indians. The Mexicans sent troops to take the cannon, but it had been buried in a peach orchard for preservation. When a Mexican officer and his troops arrived the cannon was dug up, mounted on oxcart wheels, loaded with pieces of chain and scrap iron, and used to fire the first shot of the Texans' war for independence from Mexico. To taunt the Mexicans the Texans hung up a flag that reputedly bore a rough picture of the cannon and the words, "Come and take it!"

One organization that has fallen through the cracks of Texas history is the Capitol Syndicate. After the state capitol was destroyed in 1881, the 16th Legislature appropriated three million acres of land to finance a new structure. Mattheas Schnell of Rock Island, Illinois, accepted the contract in return for the land. Later the "Capitol Syndicate" was formed to get investors to provide the funds to build the capitol. Since the land the investors were to receive as payment was in the unsettled

Texas Panhandle, the syndicate established the XIT
Ranch to utilize the land until it could be sold.

A gift from an Alamo defender to one of the few
survivors is on display in the shrine of the Alamo. A
"cat's-eye" ring said to have belonged to Col. William B.
Travis was thought to have been given to him by a lady
friend, Rebecca Cummings. According to historians,
when Travis and other defenders realized they would
probably perish, they went to the room of Mrs.
Dickenson (sometimes spelled Dickerson), wife of Capt.
Almaron Dickenson, one of the Alamo defenders. Travis
had made a necklace from a piece of string and tied the
"cat's-eye" to the necklace. He is said to have placed the
string necklace around the neck of Dickenson's little
daughter, Angelina. Although Capt. Dickenson died in
the battle, his wife and daughter survived and were given
escort out of San Antonio.

Another interesting tidbit that may have slipped our
minds is the legend of the "Easter Fires" of
Fredericksburg. The town was founded in 1846 by John
Meusebach of New Braunfels. Being on the Indian
frontier, it was terrorized by Indian raids. In the spring of
1847 Meusebach successfully made a treaty with the
Comanche chiefs. The Indians gathered in the nearby
mountains and made camp to watch and make sure there
was no treachery from the whites while waiting to sign
the treaty. They built their fires to signal to one another.
Seeing the fires frightened the children of the settlement,
who were accustomed to the Indian raids. The mothers
told them that the fires were made by the Easter rabbit,
who was cooking Easter eggs in large cauldrons which

would then be colored for the occasion with dye made from flowers found on the mountains. The story of the night fires quelled the children's fear, and the legend of the Easter fires was born.

☆

Texans pride themselves in being friendly; thus the state motto, "Friendship." This motto was adopted by the forty-first State Legislature in February of 1930. It was probably selected because the name Texas, or Tejas, was the Spanish translation of the Caddo Indian word meaning "friends" or "allies." So Texans' reputation for friendliness comes not only from the attitudes of its citizens, but is well grounded in the history of Texas' first inhabitants.

☆

During the period of the Republic of Texas, notes signed by individuals promising to pay a cow and a calf passed as a ten-dollar bill, even though a cow and a calf were not worth ten American dollars!

☆

One foreign power was against the annexation of Texas into the United States. Great Britain opposed it and even contemplated force to prevent it! Britain did not want to add Texas to the British Empire, but they wanted to prevent the westward expansion of the United States to reap the commercial advantages of Texas trade. Britain's policy toward Texas so alarmed Americans that the annexation was pushed through, completed on December 29, 1845.

☆

No official documentation exists regarding the flag
Alamo defenders fought under, and there is some
discrepancy among historians in referring to it. Some
maintain that the flag used by William B. Travis and his
men was that of Coahuila and Texas—red, white, and
green, with two blue stars on the white bar. Other writers
are of the opinion that the Alamo flag was the Mexican
tri-color with the numerals 1824 on the white bar. This
is logical, as the hated union with Coahuila was one
cause of the Texas revolution, and it doesn't make sense
that Texas would fight under a flag which symbolized
that union. When they began the revolution, they did
not immediately declare for independence, but for a
liberal government as a state of the Mexican Republic.
The Texans adopted the flag of the liberal Mexican states
according to the terms of the Constitution of 1824. It
makes most sense that it was the one they fought under.

The flag flown over the Alamo during its seige in 1836 is in
dispute, however, some groups such as the New Orleans Grays,
a volunteer group, fought proudly under their own individual
banners, such as the one pictured here.

The Alamo has been used for a number of things throughout its long history. Its walls have housed troops, Indians, Tejanos, and squatters. It was San Antonio's first hospital, from 1806 to 1812. It has been used as a Masonic lodge, a jail, a commercial store, and a warehouse.

Mexican General Antonio Lopez de Santa Anna gave himself the title, "Napoleon of the West."

The first election in Texas was held in San Antonio on August 1, 1731, when appointed government officials were approved by voters.

Stagecoaches and trains were popular targets for bandits such as Sam Bass. From Indiana originally, Bass worked as a teamster around Denton. He went north to Nebraska with a cattle drive and fell in with a group of outlaws. After they held up a Union-Pacific train in the fall of 1877, Bass returned to North Texas. He planned to rob a bank in Round Rock, near Austin, in 1878, but one of the gang members alerted the Texas Rangers. When the Bass gang rode into Round Rock on July 19, Rangers confronted them, and Bass was mortally wounded in the fray.

Today, where particularly in urban areas two-car families are common, traffic laws are as much a part of our lives as eating. But Texas has had traffic laws only in this century. According to the 1992-93 *Texas Almanac*, a few automobiles were in use by 1900. By 1907 there were enough motorized vehicles on the roads that the first traffic laws were passed, limiting speeds to 18 mph and requiring that autos stop when meeting horse-drawn vehicles. Each vehicle had to be registered in the owner's home county. The state began collecting license fees for cars in 1915.

The U.S. Army Air Corps was actually born in Texas. Military aviation began in San Antonio in February 1910 when Lt. Benjamin Foulois arrived at Fort Sam Houston with seventeen crates containing an airplane, accompanied by a number of student mechanics. Foulois, assigned to the aviation section of the U.S. Army Signal Corps, had taken three flying lessons from Wilbur Wright. Because of the winter weather at the Signal Corps facility at College Park, Maryland, flight training was moved to Fort Sam Houston. Foulois had orders to assemble the plane, learn to fly it, and train others to fly it. The aircraft was a Wright brothers biplane with a wingspan of 36 feet, 4 inches, and an overall length of 32 feet, 10 inches. The power plant was a 4-cylinder, water-cooled 30.6-horsepower Wright engine. Instead of wheels, the plane was equipped with sleigh-like runners. Takeoff was aided by a sort of catapult. The plane was ready to fly by March 1. By the outbreak of World War I in 1917, the U.S. Army Signal Corps had thirty-five trained pilots and 200 training planes. Foulois proved that aviation could be a vital part of military operations and helped establish Texas as a major military aviation center. He rose to the rank of major general and became chief of the Air Corps before he retired in 1935.

☆

Some historians have written that a dispute over the size of the letters to be inscribed on the cornerstone of one of Texas' best-loved monuments threatened its construction. When the San Jacinto Monument was being built at the site of the battlefield near Houston, a flap arose when the Daughters of the Republic of Texas learned that the names of Franklin D. Roosevelt, Gov. James Allred, and Jesse Jones were to be inscribed in 1¼-inch letters, while the names of the 1836 heroes were relegated to letters of ¼ inch on the stone. A call to arms and a few meetings of the DRT at the state capitol at Austin resulted in legislation which banned the names of any living person on state monuments. On San Jacinto Day, April 21, 1937, Jesse Jones laid the cornerstone. No names were carved into the Cordova shell stone.

Jose de Escandon, the Spanish colonizer, was responsible for the first successful settlement along the Rio Grande River between present-day Laredo and Brownsville. He was born at Soto La Marina in 1700. In 1746 de Escandon was commissioned to inspect the country between Tampico and the San Antonio River, then known as "Seno Mejicano." In January 1747 he sent seven divisions into the area. In October he presented a colonization plan. Spanish red tape caused delays, but in June 1748 Escandon was made governor and captain general of Nuevo Santender. In 1749 he began establishing settlements along the Rio Grande, his first two being Camargo and Reynosa. Only two of Escandon's permanent settlements were north of the Rio Grande, Laredo and Dolores. Escandon has been given credit for starting the cattle industry in Texas in 1749 when he brought Mexican Longhorns into the fertile but mosquito-ridden lower delta area along the Rio Grande at the Gulf coast.

The bonds of matrimony, though an institution now, were more of a convenience to the early settlers of Texas. Priests were not widely available, and a couple might live together as man and wife for quite a while before a priest came along to make the union legal. Mass weddings, in which area couples gathered for one community ceremony when the priest came to town, were common practice, as was something called *bond matrimony*. This involved the couple going before the alcalde (mayor) and making a bond, written very much like the wedding vows used today. This was acceptable until a priest became available. Sometimes a long time passed before a priest came to a colony, and many couples already had children!

Bravery is no stranger to a state born in revolution, and Texans have long honored their military leaders and soldiers. The Congressional Medal of Honor was initiated in 1862 to recognize the courage and valor of the men of the Union army in the Civil War. But the honor was not reserved for "Yankee" heroism; in 1875 Sgt. John Ward of the 24th Infantry U.S. Indian Scouts received the medal after he and three companions on patrol along the Pecos River charged twenty-five hostiles.

The only battle in history in which every military participant received the Medal of Honor took place in Texas in 1874. In the "Buffalo Wallow fight" in the Panhandle county of Hemphill near the Washita River, William (Billy) Dixon, who was carrying dispatches to

Fort Supply, was surrounded by a band of Comanches and Kiowa warriors. With five companions, Dixon decided to make a stand. Four of the men were wounded before noon. Dixon located a buffalo wallow about ten feet wide some distance away and ran for it, suffering a flesh wound in the leg on the way. Dixon shouted for his comrades to come and then ran back to carry a man who had a broken leg. All day the Indians circled the men, making occasional forays. At nightfall the Indians stopped. One man was sent to find help, but failed to find the trail. Dixon found the trail and discovered a body of mounted men in the distance that turned out to be United States troops. Their commander refused them ammunition and left them, promising to notify the commander of a camp in Gray County of their condition. One man was buried at Buffalo Wallow and the five survivors were taken to Fort Supply. The five survivors received the Medal of Honor on General Miles' recommendation. After an illustrious career, Dixon became postmaster when a post office was established at Adobe Walls in 1884. He married Olive King, who for three years thereafter was the only woman in Hutchinson County! Dixon died in 1913. Since the Indian wars of the nineteenth century, sixty-five Texans have earned the highest honor for valor bestowed by an appreciative nation—the Congressional Medal of Honor. Thirty-seven of these have been awarded posthumously after recipients sacrificed their own lives for their comrades and nation.

The popularity of the name Dolores in the development of early Texas is pointed out in the *Handbook of Texas*. In 1750 Governor Don Jose de Escandon granted Vasquez Borrego fifty *sitios* (about 200,000 acres) for the founding of Dolores in what is today the southern part of Webb County, Texas. Poblacion de Dolores was the first town founded on the north (Texas) side of the Rio Grande River. The Mexican town of San Jose also was renamed Dolores when the Cannel Coal Company began mining coal along the north bank of the Rio Grande. In 1885 Charles B. Wright, president of the company, built the Rio Grande and Eagle Pass Railroad to ship the coal, and he named the San Jose station Dolores after his daughter. Established somewhat earlier was Nuestra Senora de los Dolores de la Prasidio, founded by the Domingo Ramon expedition in 1716 on the east bank of the Neches River. It was abandoned in 1719 after a French invasion of East Texas.

How long is a yard? This might be important to someone nowadays buying fabric, but it was very important to early Texas women. According to the *Southwestern Texas Historical Quarterly*, while Texas was under Spanish rule a yard was measured at 33 inches. It was not until 1832 that merchant men introduced the English measurement of 36 inches to a yard.

Of all the battles in Texas' early history, there is one that was little publicized and, as a result, has been all but forgotten. This was the "Grass Fight," an incident in the siege of Bexar that occurred the afternoon of November 26, 1835, about ten miles from San Antonio, which was then occupied by General Perfecto de Cos. A rumor had reached the Texas army that Cos had sent Domingo de Ugartechea to Matamoros for reinforcements and pay for the Mexican troops. Scouting parties were sent out to watch for Ugartechea's return. Erastus (Deaf) Smith discovered a pack train about five miles from San Antonio and reported to the Texas army what he supposed was General Ugartechea's return with a guard. James Bowie rallied about a hundred mounted men and set off in advance to intercept the Mexicans. In the ensuing fight the Texans captured some of the pack train. What was believed to be bags of silver on the pack mules turned out to be bags of grass to feed the horses of the Mexican army. In the furious fight fifty Mexican men were killed and several wounded. Of the Texans, two were killed and one was missing.

We are familiar with the expressions "two bits, four bits, six bits" when speaking of American coinage, but does anyone really know what a bit is? Early Texans had to know: some posted rates for river ferries indicated the cost for transporting one small animal, such as a hog, was one bit. As coins were a rarity in early Texas, colonists used the Spanish silver dollar known as "pieces of eight." These were minted in Mexico City in 1535 and in the 1730s. The coin could actually be cut into eight pie-shaped pieces called "bits." Each bit was worth twelve and a half cents in United States currency. When the U.S. coined the quarter, it was worth twenty-five cents, or two bits. The half dollar was worth four bits, etc. The word *peso* is actually an abbreviation for the phrase, *peso del ocho*, meaning the weight or a piece of the eight.

Texas scout and spy Erastus (Deaf) Smith is given credit for destroying Vince's bridge before the Battle of San Jacinto, which prevented reinforcements from aiding Santa Anna's army. This may have easily been Deaf Smith's most valuable effort in the Texans' behalf. He died at Richmond, Texas, on November 30, 1837, at the age of fifty.

Judging from the amount of mudslinging today's politicians engage in, it's a good thing Congress passed a law in 1840 that made dueling a capital offense and prohibited those who participated in duels from holding public office. Modern politicians do their dueling verbally in the form of debates.

There are many incidents that took place in a region of Texas known to local residents but not so familiar outside the area. They might have been part of local lore and legend, repeated from generation to generation, and have survived only through the telling. This is the case with two events that took place in the notorious Big Thicket of East Texas. Neither the Battle of Bad Luck Creek nor Kaiser's Burnout are mentioned in historical reference material, but both involve the painful pitting of neighbor against neighbor, Texan against Texan during the secession and Civil War periods of history. The central figures in both incidents were the Union sympathizers, known as "jayhawkers." Union sympathizers were not Texans who favored the Yankee cause but rather Texans who, like Sam Houston, were opposed to secession from the Union. The Battle of Bad Luck Creek took place in Hardin County one October morning in 1863. It was a battle, or rather a skirmish, which claimed only one victim, "Old Man Lilly," who found himself at the battle by a quirk of fate. He took a shot to the chest which entered his heart. The shooter was supposedly heard later saying, "If you find a man with his galluses (suspenders) busted, he's mine. I shot him."

Battle of Bad Luck Creek a Stirring East Texas Episode of Civil War Days

Pioneers of Big Thicket Country in Old Hardin County Recount History

The following is according to an article in the *Beaumont Enterprise* newspaper dated October 25, 1931, in a story told by Aunt Cordelia (or "Aunt Deal," as she is known in the Thicket). When Texas, against the hard-fought efforts of Sam Houston, joined the secession movement and left the union, there were those who sympathized with old San Jacinto. Here and there bands formed to oppose conscription, not because they favored the other side, but because they did not believe in splitting the union. They did not want to bear arms against their Texas brothers. One of these was the Collins band, well known in East Texas as Union sympathizers. Their headquarters were the two clearings surrounding the Collins homes. The bands ranged between there and a spot on the Polk County line now known as Kaiser's Burnout, or Union Wells (the older title, born of the fact that the Union adherents, really pure Southerners at heart, had dug these wells in the woods and camouflaged them with branches and leaves, so that they could get water when the creeks ran dry). Often the bands, on foot but well armed, were hard-pressed for sufficient food, especially bread and salt, and came to the Collins cabins. Their number is variously given at fifteen to twenty. The skirmish with the Union men, later dignified as a battle, has become legend, but if the battle was ever recorded on printed page, the record has never come to light. The

action began, according to the *Beaumont Enterprise,* with
Captain Bullock's formation of Bullock's Cavalry at
Woodville. They were a body of soldiery, home guards, or
Confederate militia, formed under a commission of the
Confederate government and the state to take care of
trouble and the constantly fermenting situation at home.
The nearest federal troops were across the Sabine. One of
the jobs cut out for Bullock was to capture any Union
sympathizers. Bullock's territory lay between Woodville
and the salines of the Gulf coast, so there came to his
attention this little band in Hardin County. It is a fairly
well established fact that Bullock and his men were quite
well acquainted with the Collins band, but the conscription board wanted them routed out. The band, peaceable
enough if left alone, maintained a camp near Union
Wells on the Polk County border. Up in that country was
a settler named Kaiser, an old German for whom the
county was named. The territory was a dense thicket of
woods and canebrake—an ideal hideout. Bullock
evidently saw that it was hopeless to try and invade the
place; his men were not familiar with the country, but
the Collins men surely were. Then came the browning
fall of 1863, a season of a long dry spell followed by a
brisk norther. Only torches were needed to send the
band out and southward. Fire was the only thing they
could not withstand. The militia leader ordered fire to be
set to the canebrakes and woods; it was set in sort of a
horseshoe shape in order to capture the Union band in
the center. Within a few minutes, flames fanned by the
norther and fed by the dryness caused "The Burnout," or
"Kaiser's Burnout." Another version of this story, related
in an article in *Texas Highways Magazine,* tells how a
Captain Kaiser was sent to capture deserters of the
Confederate army who were hiding in the Big Thicket
and return them to the army or shoot them. He cornered

the deserters in the Thicket and burned them out, capturing only a few and killing two. The burned area never recovered its original lushness. Other historians have written that no documentation of this episode has been found. But there are many who say that this event is the basis for the naming of Kaiser's Burnout.

Within the story of Bad Luck Creek and the "jayhawkers" are two separate pieces of trivia worth telling in detail. The first is about the naming of Bad Luck Creek, which had no name until after the battle with the militia near the Collins home in which "Old Man Lilly" lost his life. Had he not stopped and spent the night dressing a deer he had shot en route to the Collins home, he probably would not have found himself caught between the Collinses and the militia, which got him shot through the heart. It was after this, so the story goes, that the creek was given the name Bad Luck Creek.

The second bit of trivia inside the jayhawker story also involves the naming of a location—the little-known town of Honey Island in Hardin County, which according to legend figured in the jayhawker and Kaiser's Burnout story. Big Thicket legend says that the families of the Confederate army deserters fed them by taking food to a rise of ground with pine trees and hanging the food in the trees for the deserters. This area was also a popular supply depot for the hunted jayhawkers. They reported that when the jayhawkers ran short of salt, tobacco, and other necessities, they robbed bee trees and took the honey to the same rise of land and left it in exchange for whatever they needed. The little town at that location is still known as Honey Island.

During the early days of oil discovery and development in Texas, drilling crews frequently found accessibility to their work hampered by seas of mud around the drilling rigs. According to Houston wildcatter Glenn McCarthy, at times the so-called roads were hip-deep in mud on a man and belly-deep on a horse or mule. When all vehicles were so mired, drilling crews would lay logs on the roads to travel on. These were referred to as "corduroy roads."

The battle of Palo Alto, the first battle of the Mexican War, had two unique features. On May 8, 1846, twelve miles northeast of Brownsville, United States General Zachary Taylor's 2,228 men defeated a Mexican force of twice as many men. The battle was the first time in the Americas that the U.S. had used lightweight mobile artillery. Another unique feature was that the battle brought together three future presidents. Taylor became U.S. President in 1848. In his command was a young lieutenant, Ulysses S. Grant, who became 18th President of the United States. The defeated Mexicans were under command of Mariano Arista, who became president of Mexico in 1851.

With all of the atrocities laid at the feet of the Mexicans in Texas' struggle for independence, it is only fair that we mention some acts of benevolence by the Mexicans toward Texans. One of these involves Francisca Alvarez, known as the Angel of Goliad, the wife of a Mexican officer under General Jose Urrea. When she arrived with her husband at Copano on March 27, 1836, she found

Major William P. Miller with his men, who had been tied up for several hours. She ordered the cords that were restraining the Texans to be untied and refreshments be given to the prisoners. And she persuaded one of the Mexican officers to save all the prisoners he could. She personally hid several prisoners on the parapet of the fort until after the massacre. On her return to Matamoros, she also showed great kindness to Texan prisoners.

In March of 1842, after the Mexican forces tried to reassert their claim on Texas by moving into San Antonio and demanding its surrender, President Sam Houston called an emergency session of the Texas Congress. Fearing that the Mexicans might move on Austin, Houston had the meeting moved to Houston. Historians write that the citizens of Austin, fearing that Houston wanted to make his namesake city the permanent capital of the Republic, formed a local vigilance committee. When officers prepared to remove some of the papers, the archives were packed into boxes, and a guard was placed over them. At the end of December 1842, President Houston sent a company of Rangers to Austin to remove the archives to Washington-on-the-Brazos with orders not to resort to bloodshed. The Austin vigilantes were unprepared for the raid and the Rangers were successful in their mission, loading the archives into wagons and driving away, but not before being fired upon by a cannon set off by Angelina Eberly. On January 1, 1843, the vigilance committee seized a cannon from the arsenal and overtook the wagon at Kenny's Fort on Brushy Creek. Only a few shots were fired, the Rangers giving up the papers to avoid bloodshed.

☆

The first Baptist church on Texas soil was organized at Washington-on-the-Brazos by Z.N. Morrell in 1837. The adoption and signing of the Texas Declaration of Independence was done in the blacksmith shop of Noah T. Byers, an early settler in whose shop the Congress met temporarily. Byers was an ordained minister in the Baptist church and was given credit for founding a number of Baptist churches as well as other Baptist institutions. He was a member of Texas' first Baptist church at Washington-on-the-Brazos.

Although much has been written about the Black Bean incident (see Truth is Stranger than Fiction), what happened to the remains of the seventeen shot as a result of drawing the black bean is almost lost in the footnotes of history. The bodies of the men were brought back from Mexico and buried at what is now known as Monument Hill, near LaGrange, Texas.

The first case of bloodshed in the relations between Texas and Mexico took place on June 26, 1832, in what is known as the Battle of Velasco. This was the first incidence of colonial resistance to Mexican authority. Henry Smith and John Austin, in charge of Texans who had gone to Brazoria to secure a cannon to use against the Mexican forces at Anahuac, went up against Domingo de Ugartechea, commander of the Mexican fort at Velasco, who tried to prevent passage of the vessel carrying the cannon. The Texans numbered between one hundred and one hundred fifty. The Mexicans numbered between ninety-one and two hundred. Ugartechea and his garrison were forced to surrender when his ammunition was exhausted. Texan casualties were ten killed and eleven wounded. Of the Mexicans, five were killed and sixteen wounded.

The coat of arms for the Republic of Texas was established by an Act of Congress on January 25, 1839. It was declared to be a star of five points on an azure background encircled by olive and live oak branches. The national seal bore the arms encircled by the words "The Republic of Texas." The Constitution of 1845 provided for the same seal with the words changed to "The State of Texas."

Reprinted from the 1996-1997 Texas Almanac published by the A.H. Belo Corporation.

The Battle of San Jacinto resulted in Texas' independence from Mexico, but that did not mean Mexico gave up her claim to Texas. It was not until the Treaty of Guadalupe Hidalgo was signed after the Mexican-American War in 1848 that Mexico relinquished her claim to Texas and the boundary between the United States and Mexico was established as the Rio Grande River.

It is doubtful that many of us know where in Texas the "grave of the Confederacy" is located. The story behind this thought-provoking item is as follows: In May of 1865, just after the collapse of the Confederacy, General Joseph Orville Shelby, commander of the Missouri Raiders, who were stationed in Texas at the time of Robert E. Lee's surrender, led his brigade across Texas and into Mexico. This was known as the Shelby Expedition. Shelby had refused to surrender. His troops were estimated variously at between 3,000 and 12,000. When some 1,000 reached Piedras Negres, which is across from Eagle Pass, they buried their Confederate flag at the Rio Grande in a ceremony which became known as "the grave of the Confederacy incident."

At one time, believe it or not, Texans were on the side of Santa Anna. In October of 1832 delegates from sixteen Texas districts met at San Felipe and voted their support for a revolutionary trying to overthrow the Mexican government. His name: Antonio Lopez de Santa Anna.

The Battle of San Jacinto was a pivotal one for Texas as it led to nationhood, then statehood, but this weighty event actually took place in a brief amount of time— eighteen minutes. The Texans lost only nine men, and thirty-four were wounded.

Although little has been written about the capture of the "Napoleon of the West," as Santa Anna liked to call himself, his positive identification the time he was captured can be credited to his own troops. According to the *Handbook of Texas*, "Santa Anna, who had disappeared during the battle, was discovered by James A. Sylvester and others on April 22 and was recognized by the

Mexican prisoners when he was brought into camp." The Texans were not sure they had captured Santa Anna at first because of his less-than-grandiose dress. His identity was revealed by the Mexican prisoners, whose homage gave him away.

Of all the various groups of settlers who made, or attempted to make, Texas their home, two French groups because of their uniqueness deserve special attention. The pirate Jean Lafitte set up a republic in April 1817 on Galveston Island that grew to more than 1,000 people by 1818 and was abandoned in May of 1820. And a group of Napoleonic exiles under Charles Lallemand in 1818 tried to settle at Champ d'Asile on the Trinity River near present-day Liberty, but the settlement had to be abandoned because of food shortages and threats from Spanish authorities.

Texas' first civil rights march was prompted by the shameful actions of the first Legislature elected after the 1866 Constitutional Convention during the days of Reconstruction. The Legislature passed a law allowing blacks to testify in court cases only if the case involved other blacks; segregating blacks on public transportation; prohibiting blacks from holding public offices, serving on juries, or voting; and prohibiting blacks from marrying whites. Seeking their civil rights, blacks began to organize chapters of the Loyal Union League. The state's first civil rights march involved one black man in Webberville, near Austin, who in 1868 carried an American flag and a saber and led the town's black voters to the polls to vote in an election on whether or not to hold another Constitutional Convention.

The last engagement between the Cherokee Indians and whites in Texas occurred July 15-16, 1839, in what is known as the Battle of the Neches. The Cherokees, with a reputation of being a peace-loving and nonviolent tribe, had their warriors mobilized by Chief Bowles to prevent their expulsion from their lands along the Angelina River after President Mirabeau B. Lamar ordered the tribe to be removed from Texas. Bowles, who had a close relationship with Sam Houston, had offered to have the Cherokees war against the wild tribes of West Texas. Bowles was killed in the battle. The battle was fought a few miles west of Tyler near the Neches River. The first day's engagement was in what is now Henderson County. The second day's activity took place in what is now Van Zandt County. Texan troops numbering about 500 engaged the Indian army of 700-800. The Indians were routed, although pursuit continued until July 24. Indian Chief Bowles remained on the field of battle on horseback wearing a handsome sword and sash given to him by President Sam Houston. He was shot and killed by the Texans; the tribe was expelled from East Texas, and Indian trouble in the settled portions of that area ended. But even today, the Battle of the Neches refuses to die. A "war of words" is kept at the boiling point by descendants of the Texas Cherokees, who claim the battle was not a heroic military action but a wanton massacre of Cherokee men, women, and children who made up the Cherokee Indian village at the site of the battle. As late as November 1993, these descendants were making an effort to have the small granite marker that was placed at the site and engraved with a description of the events changed to reflect what, in their opinion, is the true story of the important battle.

The story of the Alamo is almost biblical in significance to Texans, however few know what happened to the bodies of the 189 defenders who died there. The most accepted account is that Santa Anna ordered the bodies collected, piled in a heap, and burned. Only the body of Gregorio Esparza, the brother of a Mexican soldier, was spared and given a separate burial at San Fernando church. There are several versions of what happened to the ashes after the bodies were burned. According to the *Texas Almanac*, they were buried by remnants of the Texas army about a month and a half later, but no one knows where. Another report says that "Colonel Seguin, with his command stationed at Bexar, paid the honors of war to the remains of the heroes of the Alamo." According to that report, "the ashes were found in three heaps. The two smallest heaps were collected and placed in a coffin covered in black, with the names Crockett, Travis, and Bowie engraved on the lid, and taken to Bexar and placed in the parish church." The remaining ashes were collected and buried after a ceremony.

Following his defeat at San Jacinto, Santa Anna was held prisoner at one of Texas' oldest towns, Velasco, at the mouth of the Brazos River, where, ironically, Stephen F. Austin landed his first colonists in 1821.

☆

In 1528, when Cabeza de Vaca's boat was wrecked in a storm, its occupants were cast ashore on a Texas coastal island which the Spaniards called "Malhado." While authorities differ on which island it was, several believe it was Galveston Island.

Texas once had to sell part of her navy to pay repair bills. The sixty-ton schooner *Liberty*, mounting four or six guns in May of 1836, under the command of Captain George W. Wheelwright, carried the wounded Sam Houston to New Orleans. The ship was detained in that city for repairs and had to be sold to pay the bill.

The "whip-handle dispatch" refers to a group of letters sent from Matamoros, Mexico, to Texas in 1836. The letters, which were hidden in a hollow whip handle, were written to warn the Texans that a large number of Mexican troops might invade Texas in the summer of 1836. The dispatch resulted in the issuance of a circular calling for the enlistment of the militia on June 20, 1836.

Every now and then, in her older years, my mother would go on a story-telling binge. And times she seemed to recall most were those growing up in the 1890s and early 1900s in the rural community of Big Valley on the Colorado River near Goldthwaite, Texas. A common pastime among young people then was to go "Kodaking" on a Sunday afternoon. This meant simply taking the family's box camera (usually made by Kodak, as most were then) and going with friends to some scenic spot to spend the afternoon and take pictures of each other. One story she told many times was about the Sunday when she and the neighbor girls went up on the mountain "Kodaking" and were not aware until the negatives were developed that there was a big rattlesnake sunning himself on the large boulder they were using as a backdrop!

The restored remains of the original 1835 San Jacinto flag is the oldest artifact in the state capitol of Texas. It hangs behind the Speaker's desk in the House Chamber. The flag features a female figure holding a sword over which is draped a sash or ribbon bearing the slogan "Liberty or Death."

The last battle in the Dallas/Fort Worth area between settlers and Indians was fought by an expedition under command of General E.H. Tarrant in what was known as the Battle of Village Creek. The battle was fought in May of 1841 where Village Creek crosses Highway 80 near present-day Arlington. One casualty of the battle was John B. Denton, for whom Denton County was named. The destruction of the village at Village Creek helped make Tarrant County safe for Anglo settlement.

For a time, Texas and the Philippines bore the same name. Nueves Filipinas (New Philippines) was the name for Texas about 1716. Don Martin de Alercon was appointed governor of the New Philippines. Yoakum's *History of Texas* shows a map of Spanish Texas with the New Philippines clearly marked.

Dr. N.D. Labadie, who fought in the Battle of San Jacinto, wrote in the *Texas Almanac* of 1859 that General Houston tried to stop the Texans from the "orgy of wanton slaughter" that the battle turned into because of the Mexicans' "ineptness, and being overpowered with no direction."

There was a time when knighthood was bestowed upon certain Texans. Sam Houston created the Order of San Jacinto between 1842 and January 1843 during his second term as President of the Republic of Texas. In 1939 the Sons of the Republic of Texas revived the Order of San Jacinto so that they could honor distinguished Texans.

Sophia Porter was the widow of Holland Coffee of Coffee's Station fame. She married Coffee in 1837. They built their home, Glen Eden, near Preston Bend on the Red River. After Coffee was killed at his trading post, Sophia married Major George Butts in 1846. During the Civil War Sophia Butts forded the Red River to warn Colonel James Bourland of the approach of federal scouts. This earned her the title, "a woman Paul Revere." After Major Butts' death, Sophia married Judge James Porter, a former Confederate officer from Missouri. They returned to Glen Eden, where she lived until her death in 1899.

CONFEDERATE LADY PAUL REVERE
SOPHIA PORTER
(1813–1899)

SETTLED 1839 AT GLEN EDEN, A SITE NOW UNDER LAKE TEXOMA (N OF HERE). HER HUSBAND, EARLY TRADER HOLLAND COFFEE, BUILT FINE HOME. GUESTS INCLUDED ROBERT E. LEE, ULYSSES S. GRANT, OTHER ARMY OFFICERS, 1845–60. DURING CIVIL WAR, WINED AND DINED PASSING FEDERAL SCOUTS, FOUND OUT THEY WERE SEEKING COL. JAS. BOURLAND, CONFEDERATE DEFENDER OF TEXAS FRONTIER. WHILE GUESTS WERE BUSY, SHE SLIPPED OUT, SWAM HER HORSE ACROSS ICY RED RIVER, WARNED COL. BOURLAND, HELPED PREVENT FEDERAL INVASION OF NORTH TEXAS. (1965)

This historical marker is near Preston Bend Cemetery, where Sophia Porter and her husband Holland Coffee are buried

Texas' victory of independence from Mexico may have influenced the formation of another republic. Not much is written about the Republic of the Rio Grande because

it existed for less than a year, but an effort on the part of the federalist leaders in Tamaulipas, Nuevo Leon, and Cohuila to break away from the centralist government of Mexico in 1840 formed a new confederation that included part of Texas. Since 1835, when Antonio Lopez de Santa Anna, then a centralist, became president of Mexico, leaders throughout the nation had attempted to force a return to the federalistic Constitution of 1824. The sentiment was particularly strong in the northern states of Mexico, and when they failed to succeed at their quest, the northern federalists set out to win independence from the Mexican Republic. Texas' recent success at winning de facto independence probably influenced their action. On January 17, 1840, they convened at Laredo, Texas, and declared independence from Mexico and staked their territorial claim on the areas of Tamaulipas and Coahuila north to the Nueces and Medina Rivers, respectively. This became literally a land between two lands. After several military confrontations, on November 6, 1840, the federalists capitulated, and the republic, which had lasted less than a year, came to an end.

The Guadalupe bass, a member of the sunfish family, was named the official state fish of Texas by the 71st Legislature in 1989.

The Fifty Cent Act advocated by Governor O.M. Roberts was approved by the Texas Legislature July 14, 1879. It provided for selling Texas public land at fifty cents an acre, one half of the proceeds to be used for paying the public debt, and the other half to be used to establish a public school fund. The Act opened to settlement about fifty-two West Texas counties, out of which 3,201,283 acres were sold for $1,600,645.55. The Act was repealed in January 1883.

While most people are familiar with the term "greenbacks," there was a time when the Republic of Texas printed "redbacks." Because of its heavy indebtedness, the Republic of Texas resorted to offering interest-bearing notes to raise funds to retire its indebtedness. In 1840, however, noninterest-bearing notes were issued. These were called redbacks.

Santa Anna's life was spared after he was captured and identified at San Jacinto, and he was brought before Sam Houston, whose men wanted to execute him immediately. Texas historians have written that since Santa Anna and Houston were both Masons, Santa Anna gave the Masonic "distress signal" and Houston intervened to spare his life.

The Coke-Davis controversy was not limited to the common man in Texas, as this display of politicians using force will indicate. The gubernatorial election of 1873, in which Richard Coke defeated E.J. Davis 85,549 votes to 42,663, had been characterized by fraud and intimidation on both sides. The Supreme Court held that the election was illegal, and Davis, the Republican incumbent, maintained that he had a right to finish out his four-year term. Nevertheless, the Democrats secured keys to the second floor of the capitol and took possession. Davis reportedly had troops stationed on the lower floor. The Texas Rifles, summoned to protect

Davis, were converted into a sheriff's posse and protected Coke. The tense situation went on from January 16 to 17, 1874, until a telegram from President Ulysses S. Grant indicated that he did not feel warranted to send out federal troops to keep Davis in office. Coke's inauguration restored Democratic control in Texas.

In 1840 James Hamilton, commissioned by the Republic of Texas to negotiate foreign policy, was successful in making treaties with England concerning commerce and slave trade, making Texas the only state with which England had separate and ratified treaty relations. The treaties were ratified in 1842.

The "Semicolon Court" is a historic and derisive appellation given to the Supreme Court of Texas during Reconstruction in Texas. The name was given because the court invalidated the general election of 1873 based on the placement of a semicolon in Section 6, Article 3 of the Constitution of 1869.

While it is generally believed that Texas' secession from the Union in 1861 was the state's only experience with secession, the formation of Rockwall County proves this is not so. Settlement of Rockwall County began in 1846 when the area was part of Kaufman County. Because of inconvenience in reaching the county seat, settlers decided to secede from Kaufman County and organize their own county. It was, according to local historians, a bloodless secession. By setting up their own county, the settlers made it convenient to handle county business.

The separate county was organized in 1873, and Rockwall was made county seat.

The Fredonian Rebellion began December 16, 1826, when Benjamin Edwards and some thirty followers angered by controversy between Mexican authorities and emprasario Hayden Edwards rode into Nacogdoches under a flag inscribed "Independence, Liberty, and Justice," seized the Old Stone Fort, and proclaimed the Republic of Fredonia. On December 21 the Fredonians made an agreement with Richard Fields and Doctor John Dunn Hunter dividing the area of Texas between the Fredonian Republic and the Indians in return for Indian help in the rebellion. Local inhabitants of Nacogdoches were opposed to the movement, but they did fear the results of Indian cooperation, and many of them began to retreat across the Sabine River. The Indian alliance did not materialize, and the Fredonians' appeal to the United States and to the inhabitants of Stephen F. Austin's colony were fruitless. The Mexican officers and militia, including members of Austin's colony, reached Nacogdoches; the revolutionists fled and crossed the Sabine River on January 31, 1827.

Among the earliest to fence North Texas lands were William Ikard and his brother, E.F. Ikard, who bought ranchland in Archer and Clay Counties in the late 1800s. An English translation of the history of the German-Catholic community of Windthorst in Archer County relates that in 1891, 75,000 acres of ranchland that had previously belonged to E.F. Ikard was purchased for the purpose of establishing a German-Catholic settlement.

Thomas V. Munson of Denison is considered the father of the grape industry in Texas. In the 1890s Munson developed many new varieties of grapes and was responsible for many grapevine cuttings being shipped to France, where they were credited with saving the French vineyards from destruction by the grape phylloxera.

The vineyards at Delany Vineyards and Winery in Grapevine, Texas, is an excellent example of Texas' grape-growing capability. Delany's is one of several producing vineyards in the town that comes by its name honestly. Other vineyards can be found in West Texas and the Hill Country.

During the Civil War, the Texas municipalities of Galveston, Beaumont, Gonzales, Hallettsville, Helena, Independence, and Victoria played a unique role in the postal system: they issued their own postal stamps. Neither the Republic nor the state of Texas issued postage stamps, but during the Civil War local stamps known as "Confederate postmaster's provisions" were issued by individual municipalities in Texas. These local stamps were not authorized by the Confederacy, but because the Confederate government could not supply its own stamps until October 1861, cities throughout the South, including some Texas cities, produced their own stamps for prepayment postage. The Gonzales stamps are of particular interest because the advertising labels of Law and Colement bookseller and druggists were pressed into service when Law was postmaster of Texas.

One-hundred-year-old Effie Thomas has a story about drunk driving in her hometown of Wills Point, Texas, in 1903. She relates how, although there were no automobiles in that town yet, her father, who was city marshal, forbade her to play in the street in front of her house which ran from the center of town out to the country. There were three saloons in Wills Point, and errant citizens who "tanked up" on "John Barleycorn" would whip their horses into a run as they drove their wagons and teams home from town. This overindulgence created a hazard for all in the vicinity. With the advent of Prohibition, Effie adds, the problem ended.

According to the *Wills Point Chronicle* of October 28, 1909, Robert McLeod of Van Zandt County, by cutting a cotton cord, caused a President of the United States to make an unscheduled speech. This enabled hundreds of Texans for the first time in their lives to see and hear the President of the United States. On October 24, 1909, residents of Wills Point and the territory for miles around came to town to see William Howard Taft as he stopped there on his tour of Texas. The president's private car was attached to the regular 10 o'clock Texas and Pacific "Cannon Ball," which was a regular train through town. Even more important, the Chief Executive had promised to greet the people of the town at the station. When it was decided to make a "special" of the train, the railroad gave orders cutting out all the stops along the way. This was not learned in Wills Point until a large crowd had gathered in hopes of seeing and hearing the president. There was a semaphore atop the station which signaled the engineers whether to stop or continue through town, and it was in the vertical (go) position. A bystander who was an engineer was overheard saying "Too bad if someone cut the cord which allows the semaphore to drop from the vertical position to the horizontal position." A plucky Bob McLeod of Van Zandt heard him and, showing no fear of railroad officials, climbed atop the station and as the train pulled into the yards, cut the cotton cord. This allowed the signal to drop to the "stop" position; the engineer promptly stopped the train, and the President came forth and made a brief speech. Effie Thomas, who was born in Wills Point, said that when Taft asked "What town is this?" and someone replied "Wills Point," the President replied, "It sure is a town with a will, all right!"

Many have cursed the Texas "black gumbo" soil for its bogging effect while trying to work it into some form of civilized use. But according to historians, the sticky black dirt had its virtues, among those the invention of the disc harrow and disc plow, two of agriculture's most valuable farm implements. Norwegian immigrant Jens Ringness encountered the miring mud and in the process of pushing his wagon out of the muck noticed the cupping action of the wheels. This gave him the idea for what became the disc plow and disc harrow. He developed working models of the implements and went to Washington to see the patent office about the inventions. While on a trip in 1872, Ringness died mysteriously, and it is believed that his death was due to the fact he was carrying a large sum of money. Other references say that Ringness died from an illness. His family failed to follow up on his patent, and another plow company manufactured the disc plow and disc harrow, robbing the Norwegian inventor of the fame and fortune associated with his contribution to agriculture.

Some events in Texas history have been edited or "censored" when teaching them to schoolchildren because they were deemed inappropriate for young ears. One of these is the story of how Santa Anna lost the battle at San Jacinto. The "siesta theory," which I was taught in school, was that the Mexican leader was caught napping when the Texans attacked. The fact of the matter is that the Mexican general, living up to his reputation as a lady's man, was occupied with the young and beautiful Emily Morgan, a mulatto servant whom he had captured and put into service in his household. The girl, whom history has indicated was loyal to the Texans' cause, was later immortalized in the song, "The Yellow Rose of Texas." Therefore Santa was not merely caught napping—worse, he was caught literally with his pants down!

People

Folks around the world have a Texan, Daniel Haynes, to thank for a good night's sleep. In the 1880s, the Austin County settler invented the process and the machinery for manufacturing the cotton mattress. This was the forerunner of today's modern bedding. Haynes named his company for the town where he developed the machinery—Sealy, Texas. Thus began the Sealy Mattress Company.

Before Texas newspaper subscribers depended on Ann Landers or Dear Abby for their advice to the lovelorn, many newspapers, including the *Dallas Times Herald*, carried a popular columnist who dispensed her syndicated wisdom in matters of the heart. Her name was Dorothy Dix, the pen name of Elizabeth Merriweather Gilmore. Gilmore was born in Montgomery County, Tennessee, in 1870 and died in 1951. She was at one time editor of the women's department at the *New Orleans Picayune* newspaper and authored many books. She wrote her very popular column in the "golden years" of her life, which perhaps better qualified her for the sage advice she offered.

Texas has produced many well-known and famous people. Dale Evans, wife of film star Roy Rogers, was born in Italy, Texas; Charles E. (Rosie) Rosendahl, an Admiral in the U.S. Navy, was born in Cleburne, Texas. Rosendahl was a dirigible pilot and helped make the giant airships a valuable part of the United States fleet. And although C.W. Post was not born here, the inventor of Post Toasties and other breakfast cereals as well as the drink Postum made his home in Texas in the 1880s. He founded the city of Post in Garza County.

A prominent Texas family is responsible for putting two words in the dictionary. *Gobbledygook*, coined by U.S. Representative Maury Maverick after the gobbling of turkeys, means "inflated, involved, and obscure verbiage characteristic of the pronouncements of officialdom," according to *Webster's New Collegiate Dictionary*. In a biography of the Congressman it was explained that in 1944 Maverick, while serving as chairman of the Smaller War Plants Corporations Committee, wrote a memo to his staff in which he told them to stay away from wordy, unintelligible correspondence. "Don't use so much gobbledygook." This memo was picked up by the press and printed in other publications, and the word soon became synonymous with pompous or wordy talk. Maury's grandfather, Samuel A. Maverick, a cattle owner who did not brand his calves, is responsible for giving the word *maverick* its meaning. Again referring to the dictionary, maverick means "an unbranded animal especially a mother's calf formerly customarily claimed by the first one branding it." A second meaning is "a refractory or recalcitrant party or group" which "initiates an independent course." It has been written that when Samuel Maverick, a signer of the Declaration of

Independence, went into the cattle business before the
Civil War, he branded his stock with his MK brand. He
failed, however, to brand his initial herd. Thereafter,
when a cowboy stumbled across an unbranded steer he
considered it Maverick's, or a *maverick*.

Francis Scott Key, who wrote the words to the "Star
Spangled Banner," was employed as defense council for
Sam Houston. In 1832, before coming to Texas, Houston
was insulted by a U.S. Congressman while serving as an
Indian Agent in Washington. Houston encountered the
Congressman on the street and assaulted him with his
ever-present hickory cane. The Congressman filed
charges against Houston, and Houston hired Key to
defend him. Houston was found guilty and reprimanded.

Texans have a reputation for their wealth and for doing
things in a big way. An example of this is a story about
Dallas oilman Clint Murcheson Sr. It is said that
Murcheson lost 12,000 acres of land on Matagorda
Island to a business associate by merely flipping a coin.

After the transcontinental railroad was completed in the
1880s, passenger travel from Texas to California via the
Southwestern states was a long, dusty, uncomfortable
trip, with few opportunities for eating or resting from the
tiring, upright seats. That was alleviated when Fred
Harvey made a contract with Santa Fe Railroad officials
to build restaurants and hotels at various stops along the
way in Texas and throughout the Southwest. This made
train travel more marketable, and Harvey Houses, as

they were called, became a household word among train travelers.

Texas has produced three Miss Americas: Jo Carroll Dennison of Tyler; Phyllis George of Denton; and Shirley Cothran of Fort Worth.

John Warne "Bet-A-Million" Gates was a barbed wire tycoon from Texas who risked his fortune in the 1870s betting that barbed wire would change the course of the frontier. Gates gave a demonstration in front of the Hord Hotel on the southwest corner of the main plaza in San Antonio to show the effectiveness of barbed wire. He made a corral with the wire and filled it with longhorn cattle. The barbed wire successfully contained the livestock and resulted in more orders for the wire than the factory could fill. The wire did, indeed, prove to make a difference in the old frontier and made "Bet-A-Million" Gates a rich man; after he was refused partnership in the company he went into business for himself.

Some Texans are better known by their professional names: Francis Octavia Smith (Dale Evans); Tulia Ellice Finklea (Cyd Charisse); and Baldemar Huerta (Freddy Fender).

James Stephen Hogg was the first native-born governor of Texas. He was elected governor in 1890 and retired in 1895 after serving two terms.

An Austin woman, Jamie Stewart, made her mark in the world sports records in 1976 by being the first Texas woman to swim the twenty-one-mile English Channel. She made the crossing in fourteen and a half hours.

One early Texas settler should not go unrecognized, if only because of his strange deathbed request. Captain James "Brit" Bailey came to Texas before Stephen F. Austin and settled near the Brazoria River in what is today called Bailey's Prairie in Brazoria County. Historians say that on Bailey's deathbed he told his wife that he had "never bowed, or stooped to any man, nor had he been knocked down." He then requested that he be buried feet down, so no man could ever look upon his grave and say, "There lays old 'Brit' Bailey, flat on his back." Honoring his request, upon Bailey's death in 1833 his wife had a vertical grave dug and had Bailey's casket lowered into it feet first!

One of America's best-known and most versatile athletes, Babe Didrikson Zaharias was born Mildred Ella Didrikson in Port Arthur, Texas, on June 26, 1914. She attended school in Beaumont, then in 1930 moved to Dallas, where she started her track and field career. The three-time basketball all-American, Olympic gold medalist, and world-class golfer was named by the Associated Press as Woman Athlete of the Year six times. Babe got her nickname as a young girl because of her unusual athletic ability at a time when Babe Ruth was the best-known athlete in America. She became a professional and went into show business for a short time, singing and playing the harmonica. In 1953 Babe underwent an operation for cancer, and few believed she would return to sports; however she came back to win several professional golf tournaments, including the National Open. Her career was cut short when she died of cancer in 1956 at the age of 42. She was buried in Beaumont, which is now the home of the Babe Didrikson Zaharias Museum.

Some refer to the nationally renowned Judge Roy Bean, "the law west of the Pecos," as "the hanging judge" because of his strict method of dispensing frontier justice. But it is highly unlikely that the proprietor of the Jersey Lily Saloon at Langtry, Texas, was deserving of this severe title, for he had had his own experience with the rope. He told the story of how once when he was involved with a Mexican girl, a rival strung him up to a tree. The girl succeeded in cutting him down in time to save his life, but the experience left him with a stiff neck and an aversion to this form of punishment.

General Robert E. Lee, hero of the South during the Civil War, had connections to the Lone Star State. On March 15, 1860, Lee left San Antonio for duty at Fort Ringold, located on the Rio Grande River at Rio Grande City. His objective was to capture Juan Cortina, the Mexican bandit. Although experienced in Indian warfare, Lee was unsuccessful in trapping his slippery foe. He did, however, secure a promise from Mexican officials that they would effect the arrest.

An interesting bit of trivia is about a Texan who held the title of Queen. It was a dubious honor, for the exact title as recorded by historians was "Outlaw Queen of the

Indian Territory." Belle Starr was born Myrabelle Shirley in 1848 in Missouri. At the end of the Civil War, her family moved to Scyene, Texas, and settled on a farm in the community east of Dallas. She eloped with a horse thief, Jim Reed of Missouri. Reed, who was also a stagecoach bandit, was wanted in connection with several killings. He was killed resisting arrest in August of 1874. During the next few years his widow did some roving around and was accused of disposing of livestock stolen by her male friends. In 1880 she want to the Indian Territory and married a Cherokee Indian by the name of Sam Starr, and their place became headquarters for a band of ruffians. In February of 1883 both Sam and Belle were convicted of horse theft and sent to prison. Belle was killed by an unknown gunman on a road near her home in 1889.

The first black known by name to cross the Rio Grande north into Texas was Estavan (Steven). He was also known as Estevanico, Stephen the Moor, and Black Stephen, and was the companion of explorer Cabaza de Vaca during his year-long journey through Texas from 1528 to 1536.

Texans of Mexican heritage are generally known as Mexican-Americans; in some other areas Americans of Mexican descent are called Chicanos; early Texans of Mexican descent were called Tejanos. Many of the Tejanos played important roles in settling Texas and helping her to gain her independence from Mexico. A few of our Tejano heroes were Juan Seguin, Gregorio Esparza, and Lorenzo De Zavala. It should be noted that

Esparza fought in the Alamo on the side of Texas, while his brother fought with Santa Anna's army.

The pages of early Texas history seem to be saturated with heroes. Since the Indian Wars of the nineteenth century sixty-five Texans have earned the highest honor for valor bestowed by an appreciative nation: the Congressional Medal of Honor. Thirty-seven of the medals were awarded posthumously after recipients sacrificed their own lives for their comrades and their nation.

Two Texas heroes are associated with buildings in the shape of steamboats. The home of Sam Houston in Hunstville was called Steamboat House because it was constructed in the shape of a riverboat. The Admiral Nimitz Museum in Fredericksburg, honoring World War II fleet hero Chester Nimitz, is housed in his grandfather's old Steamboat Hotel. It, too, was built in the shape of a riverboat.

One of Texas best-known artists and rather eccentric citizens was sculptress Elizabet Ney. According to the *Texas Almanac*, Austin, Texas, was turned on its ear by the arrival of the 59-year-old German-born sculptress in 1892. A former confidant of European nobility, she and her husband, Dr. Edmund Montgomery, had lived near Hempstead since 1873. Contrary to tradition, Ney retained her maiden name, and she raised local eyebrows by doing such things as wearing bloomer-type slacks and when one of her children died, cremating his remains in the fireplace of her limestone home, Liendo. Ney was known for her statues of noted Texas figures—her marble statues of Stephen F. Austin and Sam Houston stand in the Texas Capitol; duplicates were placed in Statuary Hall in the U.S. Capitol.

In one of the most controversial elections in Texas history, Lyndon B. Johnson won over Coke Stevenson in the 1948 race for U.S. Senate by a margin of 85 votes out of nearly one million cast. This won for Johnson a lasting nickname, "Landslide Lyndon."

It's impossible to write much about Texans without mentioning the Texas Rangers. These distinctive peace officers are known and respected far and wide and

Ken Aten, of Garland, Texas, a friend of the author furnished this copy of an 1888 photo of Texas Ranger Company D in Realitos, Texas. The admittedly ragtag looking bunch includes Ken's great-uncle, Calvin Aten, second from left in the bottom row.

considered by many as the ultimate lawmen. Their motto, "One riot, one Ranger," is almost as legendary as "Remember the Alamo." The Texas Rangers is the oldest force of its kind in the world, but exactly when the group originated is difficult to pinpoint. In 1823 Stephen F. Austin employed ten men to serve as "Rangers," but there is no record of their operation. Again in 1826 Austin called a meeting of the representatives of the six militia districts, and it was agreed to keep twenty to thirty Rangers in service at all times. It was not until the Texas Revolution began in 1835 that the force was given legal status, when it was realized that if war came with Mexico, the danger of incursions from the west would be increased and that some provision should be made to protect that quarter. On October 17, 1835, Daniel Parker offered a resolution creating a Corps of Texas Rangers consisting of small detachments stationed on the Indian frontier. Other historians say that the Rangers were first organized November 26, 1835, when R.M. "Three-legged Willie" Williamson was commissioned a major and ordered to organize a corps of Rangers to guard the frontier from Indian attacks. As a peace officer, the Texas Ranger's commission is different from other law officers because he is authorized to operate throughout the state. He has never worn a prescribed uniform. His primary function has been one of maintaining or restoring order in situations which get beyond control of local officers, but not serious enough to justify the use of military force. The Rangers have not only protected Texans from Mexican and Indian raiders in the early days but from outlaw bands, feudists, stock thieves, and local rioters in later years.

☆

Life did not reflect well on John Wesley Hardin. One of Texas' most notorious outlaws, Hardin met his end when a constable mistook his reflection in the mirror as Hardin coming after him. Constable John Selman shot Hardin in the back of the head as he sat in the Acme Saloon on August 19, 1895. The outlaw boasted nearly thirty notches on his gun, and although he tried to stay out of trouble, he constantly ran afoul of the law. Historians say, however, that Hardin was in El Paso that particular time to act as an attorney for a relative.

John Coffee (Jack) Hays, commonly known as Capt. Jack Hays because he was a captain in the Texas Rangers, was a surveyor by profession. He was well known as an Indian fighter and is given credit for founding the city of Oakland, California. In 1849 during the gold rush, Hays led a caravan to California and for four years served as sheriff of San Francisco County. In 1853 President Franklin Pierce appointed him surveyor general of California, where he laid out the city of Oakland. Among his notable Indian fights was the defeat of the Comanche Indians from the summit of Enchanted Rock in the Texas Hill Country in the fall of 1841. Hays' last Indian fight was in Nevada in 1860. He died near Piedmont, California, in 1883.

Thousands of people from all over Texas traveled to Austin in January 1925 to see Miriam A. (Ma) Ferguson take the oath of office as Texas' first woman governor. Records indicate that many women were present to see one of their own assume the highest executive office in the state, marking another milestone in their fight for equal rights.

One of the most written-about political faux pas was made by former governor Jim Ferguson. After being embroiled in a scandal which resulted in his impeachment, on the heels of a grand jury indictment by Travis County for seven counts of misapplication of public funds, one count of embezzlement, and one count of diversion of public funds, "Farmer Jim" included the following statement in his re-election campaign speech: "Two years ago you elected the best governor money could buy. Now elect the best governor patriotism can give you." A frank critic might say this was Farmer Jim's most truthful speech.

The Texas military officer credited with coining the battle cry "Remember the Alamo" was Lieutenant-Colonel Sidney Sherman, a businessman who sold his plant and used the money to outfit a company of volunteers to fight in the Texas Revolution. After an illustrious career, Sherman died at his daughter's home in Galveston August 1, 1873.

☆

One of Texas' earliest and more able criminals was Monroe Edwards. Edwards came to Texas from Kentucky in 1827 and became involved in smuggling slaves from Cuba to Texas. His first venture brought him some $50,000, with which he bought land in Brazoria County, which he called Chenengo Plantation. Life on the plantation was not exciting enough for Edwards, however, and in partnership with one Christopher Dart he continued in slave smuggling. After several masterful swindles on the East Coast which spanned the Atlantic to Europe, Edwards was apprehended in Philadelphia and tried in New York where he was sentenced to Sing Sing Prison. He died in 1847 after being severely whipped by prison authorities for attempting to escape.

It was in a casual conversation in a Dallas retirement center that Margaret Kelly proudly told about her grandfather, George Addison Kelly, and the Kelly Plow Company, which made the "Blue Kelly" plow. The Kelly Plow Company was the only full-line plow company in the Southwest. It began in 1843 when John Stewart began making crude plows in a shop near Marshall, Texas. In 1848 he moved to Four-Mile-Branch, later known as Kellyville. George Addison Kelly joined the company in 1852. By 1854 new foundry methods were introduced, and soon the plant was not able to supply the demand for plows. The firm became Kelly and Stewart in 1858 and added other products to its line. That same year, Kelly developed the Blue Kelly plow. It was so widely used in Texas that "Kelly" and "Blue Kelly" became household words synonymous with plow. Although the prophet Isaiah prophesied that the people would "beat their swords into plowshares and study war no more," just the opposite happened with the Kelly Plow Company. During the Civil War the company beat its plowshares into "swords," becoming part of the arsenal of the Confederacy and manufacturing cast iron cannon balls. But after the war, suffering from the effects of the decline of the city of Jefferson and a plant fire in 1880, Kelly transferred the salvage to Longview in 1882. The third generation of the Kelly family managed the plant, and for over a century the one-family company has supplied plow tools to five generations of Texas farmers.

The pursuit of thieves gave Texas one of her most illustrious personages. Thomas Jefferson Rusk left Georgia in pursuit of his business partners, who had absconded with his money and fled to Texas. Rusk settled in Texas, and in 1835 he organized a company of volunteers from Nacogdoches and joined the Texas Revolution. He became inspector general for the army. Rusk was a signer of the Texas Declaration of Independence. He was elected Secretary of War in March of 1836 and later elected Chief Justice of the Texas Supreme Court. Rusk used his influence to get Texas annexed into the United States and he, along with Sam Houston, was elected to the U.S. Senate. In 1856 he was considered a political candidate for U.S. President. After his wife died in 1856, Rusk became despondent and committed suicide at his home in 1857. Rusk County is named for him.

Although Samuel Hamilton Walker was born in Maryland, he made a name for himself as a true "man of the West." After distinguishing himself as an Indian fighter in Georgia and Florida, he came to Texas in 1836 and joined the Ranger company of the well-known Captain John C. Hays, where, according to the *Handbook of Texas*, he distinguished himself as a fighter with "courage and coolness." About 1849 he was sent to New York to deal with Samuel Colt regarding the purchase of arms for the Republic of Texas. He found Colt and made certain suggestions for changes of the popular "Texas" model revolver and was largely responsible for the successfully modified pistol, known thereafter as the "Walker Colt." After participating in the Mier

Expedition, which resulted in his capture by the Mexicans. (See Black Bean Death Warrants in Chapter One, "Truth is Stranger Than Fiction.") Walker fought with General Zachary Taylor in the Mexican-American War. Walker was killed while leading a charge upon Huamantla. He was buried in San Antonio.

Frank "Bring 'em back alive" Buck was well known internationally for his lifetime of expeditions into far-off and exotic lands for the purpose of capturing and bringing back alive exotic animals, which he exhibited and filmed in his numerous motion pictures. He was born in Gainesville and attended school in Dallas. Besides the books he authored, Buck was a contributor to a number of national magazines. His expeditions went into such lands as South America, Melaya, Borneo, New Guinea, and Africa.

August Carl Buchel might be a better known name if the county named after him still existed. Buchel, who was born in Germany in 1811, was educated in Europe and knighted by the Queen of Spain before coming to Texas in 1845 and settling in Indianola. He raised a company of men in Indianola for the Mexican War and served as aide-de-camp for General Zachary Taylor. After the war, President Franklin Pierce appointed him custom collector for Port Lavaca. Buchel rose to the rank of brigadier general in the Confederate army before he was fatally wounded in the Battle of Pleasant Hill. A county was named for Buchel in 1887, but the law creating the county was repealed in 1897 and its territory included in the present Brewster County.

☆

There are many legends about one of Texas' most illustrious characters and an early proponent of Texas independence, "Three-legged Willie" Williamson. One which writers say most probably depicts Williamson's character is the legend of the case of "Colt vs. Bowie." Williamson was born in Georgia in 1804. When he was fifteen his schooling was terminated by an illness which left him a cripple for life. His right leg was drawn back at the knee; the wooden leg he wore from the knee to the ground resulted in his nickname of "Three-legged Willie." Williamson read much during his illness and was admitted to the bar before he was nineteen. He practiced law in Georgia for over a year, then migrated to Texas in 1829. He edited a newspaper for a short time and made an appeal for Texas to resist the Mexican tyranny. He was sent to the "Consultation" as a representative, and the government commissioned him a major in 1835 to organize a Ranger company. He participated in the Battle of San Jacinto. In 1836 the first Congress elected him judge of the third judicial district, and he went on to have a long and eventful political career. His district included Shelby County, where court had never been held. When locals heard that court would be held, they got up a resolution against it. Legend goes that when presented with it, Judge Williamson asked, "By whose authority was such a resolution presented?" and the presenter, who like others in Shelby County lived by the "law of the Bowie," took out his knife of the same name and laid it across the document, claiming "This is the law in this county!" "Three-legged Willie" unholstered his Colt and laid it across the Bowie knife, announcing, "And this is the Constitution that overrides the law. Call the court to order!"

☆

Alexander Horton came to Texas in 1823. He served as aide-de-camp to Sam Houston when Houston was appointed commander-in-chief of the Texas army in 1836. Horton fought as such at the Battle of San Jacinto. It is said that when he died in 1894 he was the last survivor of the Battle of San Jacinto.

☆

Bob Wills, the legendary country-and-western fiddler and swing band leader, was born in 1905 in the Limestone County town of Kosse. He lived for a while in Turkey, Texas, where it is said he made his first solo appearance playing the fiddle at age ten. Wills quit his barbering job in Turkey to go to Fort Worth to pursue his entertainment career. Bob Wills became popular as the fiddling leader of the western swing band "Bob Wills and the Texas Playboys." The Bob Wills Museum is at Turkey, where each year the town holds a "Bob Wills Day."

The coveted Heisman trophy was named for legendary football coach John William Heisman, who was the first full-time football coach and athletic director at Rice University in Houston, 1924-27.

Abner (Ab) Pickens Blocker spent his youth in ranch work and for seventeen years drove cattle up the trails from Texas to surrounding states and northward. In 1884 Blocker delivered a herd of cattle to B.H. Campbell, manager of the Capitol Syndicate's ranch in the Texas Panhandle. It is said that Blocker designed the brand that became the name XIT Ranch.

It could be said that Lucy Holcomb Pickens had the look of money. The daughter of Beverly Holcomb of Marshall, Lucy married Colonel Francis Pickens, who was later elected governor of South Carolina. As first lady of the state, and for her support of the Confederate army, Lucy was known as "Lady Lucy, Queen of the Confederacy," and her picture graced the Confederate currency.

John W. Shary was known as the father of the Texas citrus industry. He planted the first commercial citrus orchard in the Rio Grande Valley in 1911, and the town of Sharyland is named after him.

☆

Holland Coffee was known for, among other things, establishing trading posts among the Indians in Oklahoma. His most famous post was at Preston Bend on the Texas side of the Red River known as Coffee's Station or Coffee's Trading House. It was from this post that the town of Preston evolved. Shortly after he came to Texas, Coffee married Sophia Suttonfield Aughinbaugh, a divorcee (who later married Judge James Porter and was perhaps better known as Sophia Porter). She and Coffee built their plantation home, Glen Eden, at Preston. It was said that Coffee was a linguist, speaking fluently at least seven Indian languages. Coffee was killed in 1846. He was entombed in a mausoleum built by his wife just a short distance from his beloved home. With the dismantling of Glen Eden in 1942 in the creation of Lake Texoma, Coffee's body was disentombed and he was interred in a cemetery near what is today the small town of Pottsboro in Grayson County.

SITE OF THE
TRADING POST
OF
HOLLAND COFFEE

ESTABLISHED ABOUT 1837 FOR TRADE
WITH THE INDIANS OF THE RED RIVER
REGION AND THE WESTERN PLAINS •
HERE MANY WHITE CAPTIVES OF THE
RED MEN WERE REDEEMED • FROM ITS
VICINITY THE SNIVELY EXPEDITION
SET OUT FOR NEW MEXICO ON APRIL
25, 1843 • ABANDONED AFTER COFFEE'S
DEATH IN 1846

Erected by the State of Texas
1936

When Holland Coffee died in 1846 he was entombed in a mausoleum built near his beloved home, Glen Eden. When, in 1942, Glen Eden was dismantled due to the building of Lake Texoma, Coffee was interred in the Preston Cemetery near the small town of Pottsboro.

☆

Prior to his transatlantic flight between New York City and Paris, Charles Lindbergh was scheduled to report as a flying cadet at Brooks Field in San Antonio on March 15, 1924. In the interim from February to mid-March he and some others did some flying, and on several occasions Lindbergh's plane crashed, according to a biographer. On one occasion he and a friend, running low on gas, made a forced landing near the headwaters of the Neuces River. The pasture was so small that the plane couldn't take off again with both of them, so Lindbergh went up alone and landed again in the town square at Camp Wood in Real County. He attempted to take off from a street, and though he tried to miss utility poles and wires, his wing tip clipped a utility pole and his plane spun around into a hardware store. The owner refused payment for damages, saying the publicity was worth more than the cost of repairing the wall. Three years later a more improved Lindbergh made his historical solo transatlantic flight.

☆

Although you may not find D.R. (Dee) Harkey in Texas history books, he personifies the "devil-may-care" spirit that became necessary for survival in early Texas. "Dee" Harkey, a distant cousin of this author, was born March 17, 1866, at Richland Spring in San Saba County. He lived on a farm with his older brother James, who took care of him after their father died. During these times, 1869-1870, the Comanche Indians depredated in that county. In his biography *Mean as Hell*, Harkey wrote how they "killed many people and stole everything they could get their hands on." The people of the county organized a Ranger company, called a "minute company." Harkey's brother Joe was made a lieutenant, although he was very young. By 1873 the Texas Legislature had passed a law making the Rangers peace officers, and in 1880 Joe was elected sheriff. "Dee" went to work as a deputy at age sixteen. He stayed there until he was twenty, and in 1890 he moved to Eddy, New Mexico, which is now Carlsbad. There he was made a deputy U.S. Marshal and served as cattle inspector for the Cattle Raisers Association. Neither position won him many friends in that lawless territory. One of Harkey's missions was to make Carlsbad a decent and law-abiding place for settlers to live. Although his book points out that Harkey never killed anyone without giving him a chance to surrender, he tells many stories of assassination attempts on his life by those into whose outside-the-law endeavors he had interfered. One can surmise there were probably instances where he had to shoot first and ask for surrender later. Harkey definitely found use for the Indian fighting skills he learned growing up in San Saba County. "Dee" bid farewell to public service in 1911.

John Selman, the El Paso constable who shot notorious John Wesley Hardin in the back of the head, was, according to accounts in the *Handbook of Texas*, not much better than the men he disposed of. Historians wrote that he was born in Shackelford County near old Fort Griffin. After ranching in the area, Selman in 1876 became a deputy sheriff under John M. Larn, where he was involved in breaking up cattle and horse theft rings. He was, according to a later confession, involved in an extra-legal vigilance committee which lynched a number of thieves. In 1877 Larn got a contract to supply beef to the army posts at Fort Griffin. Soon there was talk about him and Selman butchering stolen cattle. In June 1878

Larn was arrested, but Selman escaped to West Texas, where his cattle rustling career continued. He was later recognized while traveling under another name and was arrested. The Texas Rangers brought him back to Shackelford County. While under indictment he was allowed to escape. In 1882 he was back in El Paso serving as a peace officer. During this time he killed several men including a former Ranger. His claim to fame came on August 19, 1895, when he shot John Wesley Hardin in the back of the head. He was acquitted on claims of self-defense. Selman was killed by a U.S. Marshal on April 6, 1896.

A family of Indian and white mixture made its mark on the map of Texas. The town of Nocona, Texas, is named for Comanche Indian chief Peta Nocona. Quanah, Texas, is named for Nocona's son Quanah Parker, a leading Comanche chief. Quanah's mother was Cynthia Ann Parker, the white woman captured at age nine and raised by the Comanches. Parker County is named for Isaac Parker, uncle of Cynthia Ann Parker, making him an uncle by marriage to Chief Nocona.

Montechena, the "German Comanche" was born Herman Lehman on June 5, 1859, near Loyal Valley in Mason County. The son of German immigrants, he had never been to school and spoke only German. At age eleven he and a younger brother, Willie, were captured by raiding Apaches. Willie escaped and returned home in a few days; Herman was adopted by his Apache captor and initiated into the rigors of Apache life. He was known as Montechena and took part in expeditions against Texas Rangers, Comanches, and white settlers.

After his captor was killed, he himself killed an Apache medicine man, spent a year alone on the plains, and then joined the Comanches. The "German Comanche" participated in Comanche raids and fought against the U.S. Cavalry. He was with the last Comanche group to surrender to the U.S. Army at Fort Sill, Oklahoma, in 1879. He was adopted, ironically, by Quanah Parker who undoubtedly felt a kinship with the white "Indian." Lehman was ultimately recognized as a white captive and forced to return to his Texas family, who thought him dead. He refused to conform to the white lifestyle, frequently startling his mother's guests by appearing in Indian dress. Lehman relearned German and English but never fully adjusted to white society. He died in 1932 and was buried in Loyal Valley.

Fray Juan de Padilla came from Spain and traveled with Vasquez de Coronado in his expedition to find gold at Cibola. It is said that de Padilla traveled as far as Quivira, and when the main body of the expedition returned to Mexico, he and some companions decided to go back to Quivira and do some missionary work. He labored in this area for a while before deciding to push further into unexplored territory. A day's journey from Quivira the party met with hostile Indians who killed the friar. The event is believed to have taken place November 30, 1544, and the state of Texas has recognized Padilla's martyrdom with a monument.

Charles A. Siringo was born February 7, 1855, in Matagorda County, Texas. After several trips on the Mississippi from New Orleans to St. Louis and back, he was employed as a cowboy and became a trail driver on the Chisolm Trail in 1876. He worked as a cowpuncher for fifteen years, working on several large ranches on the New Mexico border. After serving as a Pinkerton detective throughout the West for twenty-two years, he became a storekeeper in Kansas, where he wrote several books. He died in Hollywood, California, in 1928.

Andrew Jackson Houston, son of Sam Houston, was the oldest senator to serve in the U.S. Congress when he was appointed April 21, 1941, at age 87 to fill the unexpired term of Morris Shepard. Houston took the oath of office June 2, 1941, and served 24 days before he died in Washington, D.C. on June 26. His body was returned to Texas and buried at the San Jacinto battlefield. He served the shortest tenure of any Texan in Congress.

Arizona Senator Barry Goldwater's grandfather Mike Goldwater was instrumental in naming the Arizona town of Ehrenburg. It was named for his mining engineer and Texas Revolution fighter friend Herman Ehrenburg, a German-born immigrant to Texas. He fought with James Fannin at Goliad, escaping the massacre and returning to Germany. He eventually came back to the United States and gained wealth and distinction as a mining engineer and territorial surveyor in Arizona. Ehrenburg was robbed and killed in the Mojave Desert in California.

"Iron Jacket" (Pohebisquash) was an Indian chief and medicine man who claimed an amazing power: the ability to blow approaching missiles aside with his breath. His nickname Iron Jacket probably grew from his practice of wearing a Spanish-style coat of mail into battle. He was killed May 12, 1858, on the bank of the South Canadian River in a battle with a combined force of Texas Rangers and Brazos Reservation Indians led by John S. Ford and Shapley Ross.

Bowie County's largest baby went on to fame and fortune. The fact that he was indeed the county's largest baby might not surprise those who watched him on TV for many years in a popular Western series. Born in 1928, he weighed fourteen pounds at birth and by age twelve was over six feet tall and weighed 200 pounds. By the time he became a football star at Sul Ross University in Alpine, he was up to six feet, four inches and weighed 275. Born Bobby Don Blocker, this Texas-sized man went on to stardom as Dan Blocker, playing Hoss on the NBC series *Bonanza*.

Wiley Post, born in Grand Saline, Texas, lost an eye in an oil field accident, yet was an accomplished flyer. He and his friend Will Rogers attempted a flight to Siberia in Post's plane, the *Winnie Mae*, in August 1935 when their plane was forced down due to engine trouble near an Eskimo village in Alaska. After repairing the engine, the two attempted to take off, but the plane crashed and both Post and Rogers were killed.

Bessie Coleman, also known as "Queen Bess," was the first African-American woman to be licensed as a pilot. Born in 1892 in Atlanta, Texas, she was introduced to airplanes as a child and knew she wanted to fly. She worked in the cotton fields of Texas and in the Chicago area in a beauty parlor. Bessie was unable to find a flying school in the United States that would accept her as a student because of her race. Hard work and a dogged determination got Bessie to France, where she learned to fly and obtained her pilot's license in 1921, two years before Amelia Earhart was licensed. "Queen Bess," the barnstormer, flew as an entertainer and was doing what she loved best.

Although not a native Texan, sculptor Gutzon Borglum created his most famous work while living in San Antonio. Borglum's most monumental work was the Mount Rushmore memorial sculpture of Presidents Washington, Lincoln, Jefferson, and Theodore Roosevelt in South Dakota. The memorial was dedicated in 1927 and finished after his death by his son, Lincoln.

A political unknown in Fort Worth campaigned against the very law that kept him from voting—and won! According to the *Handbook of Texas*, W. Lee (Pappy) O'Daniel, general manager of a Fort Worth flour mill and promoter of a popular western swing radio band, entered the Democratic race for governor of Texas against twelve opponents, four of them seasoned politicians. O'Daniel was unknown in politics and unable to even vote because he hadn't paid his poll tax. Making use of another group of "hillbilly" musicians in his campaign, his platform focused on "The Golden Rule," the promise of a state pension for Texas elderly, and the elimination of the poll tax. O'Daniel won without a runoff.

If you ever found yourself involuntarily tapping your toes to the ragtime piano score of the motion picture *The*

Sting, then you have already been introduced to the Texan Scott Joplin. Known as the "king of ragtime," Joplin was born in Texarkana on November 24, 1868. Coming from a musical family, the young Joplin learned to improvise so well on the piano that a German musician volunteered to give him piano lessons at no cost. In his early teens Joplin was an itinerant pianist playing in the "red light" districts of Texas, Louisiana, and the Mississippi Valley. By 1885 he was playing in the "parlors," the only places open to black musicians in that era, of St. Louis, where a primitive sort of music called "jig piano" was in vogue. The bouncing bass line and syncopated melodic line was called "ragged-time," then simply ragtime.

General William Jenkins Worth, for whom the city of Fort Worth was named, is buried beneath a monument on the corner of Fifth Avenue and Broadway in New York City. Worth, a New York native, served in the War of 1812. Although not a graduate of the academy, he served as commandant of West Point Military Academy from 1820 to 1828. He served in the Mexican War under both Zachary Taylor and Winfield Scott and was breveted as a brigadier general for service in the Seminole War. Worth was ordered to Texas in 1848 and died there in 1849. He was returned to his native state for burial. The military establishment, Fort Worth, and the city which grew from it, were named for him.

Although the name Daisy Bradford might not be emphasized in Texas history classes, it is an important one in state history, especially to the people of East Texas. It was on Daisy Bradford's land that C. M. "Dad"

Joiner drilled the Daisy Bradford #3 oil well, which was the gusher that brought in the East Texas oil field on October 6, 1930. This was considered the greatest oil field in the world and made Joiner the "father" of the East Texas oil field; hence the nickname "Dad."

After establishing the first military aviation training school in the United States at Fort Sam Houston in San Antonio in 1910, Captain Benjamin D. Foulis' involvement in aviation in Texas was not dropped. He remained among the protagonists in America during the first years of World War I to state vehemently that America faced a great threat from Germany and should rapidly build up her own air force. Foulis, who had earlier achieved some fame in the United States by becoming America's first military pilot, stirred up great interest when he led seven U.S. aircraft of the First Aero Squadron into Ryan's pasture on November 20, 1915. The squadron's arrival in Fort Worth was only a stopover between Fort Sill, Oklahoma, and Fort Sam Houston in Texas, which was intended to become the permanent HQ of the squadron. So enthusiastic was the interest from Fort Worth citizens in this first visit of military aircraft that more than 10,000 turned out to see the squadron make its landings.

Ann Sheridan, the film actress, was born February 21, 1915, in Denton. Christened Clara Lou Sheridan, for a brief time she attended North Texas State Teacher's College, now University of North Texas. In 1933 she was one of thirty-three young women chosen to promote a Paramount film by taking part in a beauty contest. She won a screen contract, and her first five pictures were

Westerns. Publicity releases soon billed her as the "Oomph Girl" of the movies. In 1939 she was contracted by Warner Brothers and soon reached stardom.

Dale Evans, wife of Roy Rogers, got her start on Dallas radio. The popular morning variety show "The Earlybirds" was broadcast on radio station WFAA, and among the voices heard on the show was that of Dale Evans singing.

Dallas socialite Katie Rice Ripley and her husband operated the Ripley Shirt Company in the Oak Cliff section of Dallas. Ripley was sympathetic to the cause of birth control advocate Margaret Sanger. She sent shirt boxes to Sanger, who filled them with diaphragms and returned them to Ripley, who distributed them to Dallas women who wanted to use the birth control devices, a practice considered taboo at the time. Ripley started Texas' first birth-control clinic in 1935.

Josiah Wilbarger, for whom Wilbarger County is named, came to Texas from Kentucky by way of Missouri in 1827. He settled in Stephen F. Austin's colony in a bend of the Colorado River about ten miles above present-day Bastrop. In August of 1833, Wilbarger was a member of a surveying party attacked by Comanche Indians. He was scalped but still alive when found by Rueben Hornsby, who took him to his home for treatment. Although Wilbarger never fully recovered from his wounds, he lived twelve more years. He died at his home in Bastrop in 1845.

Texas-born Douglas Corrigan became internationally known as "Wrong Way" Corrigan when he took off from New York in his single-engine plane for Long Beach, California, but landed in Ireland. Corrigan was born in Galveston but moved to Los Angeles in 1922, where he became enamored with flying. He worked as an aviation mechanic and even pulled the chocks on Charles Lindbergh's *Spirit of St. Louis* on its flight from San Diego to New York before Lindbergh's pioneering solo flight across the Atlantic in 1927. By 1935 Corrigan had learned to fly and paid $310 for a secondhand 1929 Curtiss Robin monoplane, described by friends as "a crate." Only ten people had matched Lindbergh's Atlantic crossing by that time, and Corrigan longed to join them. But the U.S. Commerce Department rejected Corrigan's request for permission to fly the Atlantic. On July 17, 1938, Corrigan loaded 320 gallons of gasoline (enough for forty hours) into the tiny plane and took off from the East Coast's Floyd Bennet Field, pointing the nose straight east into a cloud bank even though he had announced that he was heading west to Long Beach. He forever claimed to be surprised at arriving at Ireland rather than California.

Visitors to Denton, Texas, might notice an elaborate marker on the southeast corner of the courthouse lawn. A close inspection will reveal that it marks the final burial site for the town and county's namesake, Captain John B. Denton. We say the *final* burial site because the story of this Methodist minister-turned-lawyer-turned-Indian-fighter reveals that the North Texas hero had been buried two times previous to his interment on the courthouse lawn! According to *Bates History and Reminiscences of Denton County* and the *Handbook of Texas*,

Captain Denton was killed in a Ranger campaign in the spring of 1841 led by General Edward H. Tarrant, for whom Tarrant County is named. The fight, known historically as the Battle of Village Creek, was against the Keechi Indians who had several villages along the creek in what is today Tarrant County. According to the Rev. Andrew Davis, a member of the Ranger company and eyewitness to the death and first burial of Captain Denton, "After the first charge was made against the Indian village, the battle was decided in favor of the Rangers. Those Indians who survived the charge retreated into the wooded area. General Tarrant called the men together and ordered John B. Denton and

Many Denton County residents attended the reburial of Capt. John B. Denton, the man who gave the county its name. After two resting places, he was buried on the Denton County Courthouse grounds in 1901. (Photo courtesy of Emily Fowler Public Library)

Henry Stout each to take a squad of twenty men and pursue the retreating Indians. A great number of them had fled into the Trinity bottoms. They used two paths leading out of their village. The Indians had secreted themselves in the dense underbrush along the river. When the company got near the Indians, they opened fire. Captain Denton was instantly killed." Rev. Davis, though a boy at the time, remembers that the men feared that the Indians would scalp Captain Denton and otherwise mutilate his body, so a squad of men was sent back to get the body. The next day they found an elevation on the south side of the creek, and using tools taken from the Indian village, they dug a deep grave and buried Denton. Although some reports say that he was buried in an unmarked grave, Rev. Davis says that the grave was marked with stones. The second burial came after Denton's friend John Chisum exhumed his remains from the creek site (just north of what is now Lake Arlington off of Highway 80 north of Six Flags) and buried them at Chisum Ranch near Bolivar (now known as the Waide place). The third burial came as a result of the writing of John B. Denton's history by the Old Settler's Association in 1900. They decided that the remains buried on the ranch near Bolivar should be moved to a more suitable place in Denton, on the courthouse lawn. One year later, Denton's remains were laid in a handsome coffin and a memorial service was held in the district courtroom. Among those in attendance were three descendants of Denton. The local newspapers reported that "following suitable honors, the coffin was borne out to the grave site on the courthouse lawn" for the third, and no doubt, final burial.

Firsts

The first public demonstration of an airplane in Texas took place February 8, 1910, near Houston when Frenchman Louis Paulhan showed off his French-made fabric-and-wood biplane.

One Texas town boasts several "firsts" in Texas. Jefferson was the first town to be illuminated by natural gas. It also had the first brewery in Texas and was the first town to produce ice commercially.

The first long-distance telephone lines in Texas were installed between Houston and Galveston in 1883. The first long-distance direct dialing in Texas was initiated in 1955.

The first movie to win an Academy Award for "Best Film" was shot in and around San Antonio. The silent film *Wings*, starring Clara Bow and Buddy Rogers, made its 1927 world premiere in the Texas Theater in San Antonio.

The first woman to fly the U.S. mail in Texas was Katherine Stinson of the famous aviation family in 1913.

Nearly forty years before the Wright brothers flew their plane at Kittyhawk in 1903, a Texan flew a fixed-wing powered airplane in Fredericksburg in 1865. Newspaper accounts reveal that Jacob Brodbeck successfully flew an airplane that he had built which was powered with coil springs. The airplane reached an altitude of tree-top heights before it crashed into a hen house, killing numerous chickens and scaring many children. Brodbeck, a teacher and inventor, came to Texas from Germany in 1846 and lived in Luckenbach.

Although tradition and history books tell us that the first Thanksgiving was celebrated by English colonists in Massachusetts in 1621, some Texans dispute this. El Paso citizens say they have written proof that the first Thanksgiving in America was celebrated a full twenty-three years earlier in their city. Based on a poem

The First Thanksgiving in APRIL

published in 1610, a decade before the *Mayflower* set sail from England, a Thanksgiving feast was held on the banks of the Rio Grande River near what is today El Paso. The poem tells the story of Spanish settlers, soldiers, and monks who had exhausted their provisions and water while traveling the Mexican desert en route to what is now New Mexico. Nearly dead from hunger and thirst, they came upon the Rio Grande and with fish and wild game supplied by Indians, they had a feast of thanksgiving and celebrated mass. El Paso citizens claim this celebration by 500 men, women, and children on April 15, 1598, was the first Thanksgiving held on American soil.

Texas housewives owe a debt of gratitude to the German immigrant Gus Baumgarten of Schulenberg. Baumgarten, a baker, invented the oven thermostat which regulates heat for baking. He became involved in a project to utilize cottonseed meal for baking; however, when government agents came to see his progress, they became more intrigued with the thermostat he had developed. As a result, they prescribed that all ovens made in the United States were to include a thermostat to regulate heat.

The first telephones in Texas were installed in 1878 in the home and office of A.H. Belo, publisher of the *Galveston News*.

The first product manufactured in Texas to be advertised on national radio was Crazy Water Crystals in June of 1932. Hal Collins, the well-known "pitch man," purchased advertising time on NBC to tout the famous elixer, a derivative from evaporating mineral water, being drunk by the gallons in hotels and pavilions in Mineral Wells, Texas. The water got its "crazy" name because it supposedly helped a mentally unstable woman whose family once camped near the well which yielded it. Hal Collins was brother of Dallas insurance executive Carr P. Collins, with whom he owned the Crazy Hotel, its trademark, and products.

Jules Bledsoe, a black man born in Waco, Texas, was the first baritone to sing the classic "Old Man River" in the 1927 New York production of *Showboat*.

The first movie filmed about the Battle of the Alamo was filmed in 1911 by Parisian filmmaker Gaston Melies. Melies was also the first person to play Colonel William B. Travis in a movie. Melies cast himself in the part.

Hollywood film star Anthony Quinn won his first Oscar for his supporting role in a movie based on the Mexican revolution and shot on location in Rio Grande City, Texas. The film was the 1952 *Viva Zapata*.

In all probability the first recorded surgical operation performed in North America was done in Texas. Spanish explorer Cabaza de Vaca, against his will, gained the respect of Indians as a medicine man and surgeon. He was the first European to practice medicine in the New World. In 1536 he removed an arrow from the chest wall of an Indian, most likely the first recorded surgical operation done in North America. He sewed up the wound and it healed.

Another Texan to whom the world owes a debt of gratitude for his invention is Gail Borden Jr. Borden, a Galveston surveyor and newspaper publisher, began inventing in the mid-1800s. In 1853 he sought a patent for processing condensed milk in a vacuum, but it was 1856 before he received British and American patents. When the Civil War brought intensified demand for such milk, his company experienced such an upsurge in sales that Borden's success was assured. Borden also invented a process for condensing various fruit juices. Millions are indebted to this Texan for taking the "bite" out of their coffee. Borden died in 1874.

Those who enjoy spicy food can thank Texas for much of their eating pleasure, as the first commercially packaged chili powder came from Texas. William Gebhardt, a German-born New Braunfels restaurateur, sold the first commercial chili powder in 1894. Before that, chili, which is the state dish, was served only when fresh chilis were available. By 1896 there was enough demand for the "eye-watering" spice that Gebhardt established a factory in San Antonio. Gebhardt added the nation's first canned chili con carne and canned tamales to his product line in 1911.

The first Texan to be categorized as a power broker and "king maker" was a quiet Austin businessman and planter named Edward Mandell House, who, nevertheless, influenced United States policy more than any American not holding office. House was the first Texan to exert influence on national politics. He had guided the election campaigns of Govs. Hogg, Culberson, Sayers, and Lanham, and he effectively controlled the forty Texas delegates to the Democratic Convention in Baltimore in 1912. He served President Wilson as an informal advisor but resisted an official position and title, preferring to work behind the scenes.

The first mass parachute drop in the world occurred April 28, 1929, at Brooks Field in San Antonio.

Air passenger service in Texas began in 1928 when Air Transport Service initiated service linking Dallas, Fort Worth, San Antonio, and Galveston. Service expanded rapidly with additional lines and routes.

The first European marriage ceremony in Texas, according to historians, took place January 12, 1687, at Fort Saint Louis, when Sieur de Barbier, who accompanied La Salle, married a young Indian maiden. De Barbier was the first colonist to marry an Indian.

During February and March 1911, the aviation section of the U.S. Army was attached to a military force along the Rio Grande River, and for the first time in American history an airplane was used for military purposes.

On February 6, 1929, the first airmail arrived in Houston.

One first that all Texans will appreciate, being keenly aware of the state's reputation for hot summers, is the development of the first automobile air conditioning by Dallasite John Mitchell of the Frigicar Company. Mitchell in 1939 installed the first automobile air conditioner in the car of the president of Packard Motor Company.

The first known Europeans to use Texas crude oil were the survivors of the De Soto expedition, who used crude oil near Sabine Pass to caulk their boats.

The first Texas oil well drilled for production was at Melrose, Texas, in Nacogdoches County in 1866. The well was drilled by Lynis T. Barret, who, unfortunately, couldn't get financial support to continue the venture because potential backers saw only poor market possibilities.

☆

One of the earliest examples of a hospital ship can be traced to Texas. As early as 1844, John Henry Bowers (Bauers), who immigrated to Texas from Germany, used the vessels *Dayton* and *Scioto Belle* as hospitals to treat yellow fever patients during an epidemic that year. Bowers earned a degree in medicine at Tulane University, joined the Texas army, and served in a military hospital in Houston. He became a protégé of Dr. Ashbel Smith.

☆

The Gladys Porter Zoo in Brownsville, Texas, has the largest collection of endangered animals in the United States.

Geography

Texas is a massive land with an abundance of natural resources and a topography as diverse as the cultures of the people who settled it. Therefore it is only natural that a multitude of state trivia falls into the category of geography. No doubt every reader could provide one or more entries of his or her own; here are just a few:

Cities in Texas are named in a variety of ways, some quite interesting. For instance, the town of Weslaco in the Rio Grande Valley was named for W.E. Stewart Land Company (WESLaCo), which promoted the land development when the Missouri-Pacific Railroad came through Hidalgo County.

Although modern cartography differs to some degree, Center City in Mills County was so named because it is the geographical center of Texas.

The Central Texas town of Lorena was named for a Civil War song which was popular with soldiers of both sides in the war. The city was named by its founder, a railroad executive who was an officer in the Confederate army.

129

He must have been very fond of the song, as he named his daughter Lorena, too!

The town of Buda (pronounced Byooda) was named for a widow who ran a hotel there. The word is a corruption of the Spanish word *viuda*, which means widow.

One Texas town got its name from its main natural resource. For many years, hundreds of thousands of Texans and residents of nearby states came to Mineral Wells to drink and bathe in its water from natural wells touted as an elixir curing everything from paralysis to baldness. The town's bath houses were crowded with people suffering all types of disorders. The magical healing water was later dehydrated and the crystals packaged and sold as a patent medicine in drug stores throughout the country.

The former town of Thurber, located in Erath County between Mineral Wells and the oil city of Ranger, attracts tourists with a restaurant in the base of a smokestack which used to be part of a coal-mining company. The town was established in 1886 as a gold-mining town, but when the gold mine became so unproductive that the company could not meet the payroll, the mine was sold to the Texas and Pacific Coal Company. After the discovery of oil in nearby Ranger, workers at Texas and Pacific went on strike for higher wages. By this time the town was called "Texas and Pacific Coal." The company had built houses, churches, and schools. After the strikes, the company converted to brick-making, then moved to Fort Worth. With no industry, the town closed in 1933. The last remaining evidence that Thurber was once an industrial town is a lone, tall smokestack that can be seen from several highways. A restaurant and gift shop were built in the base of this relic of a bygone era but have since closed.

Hereford in Deaf Smith County at one time was known as "the town without a toothache." The title was won when it was discovered that the children there had far fewer cavities and other tooth defects than in any other region. A scientific study revealed that the town's water and soil contained an exceptional amount of minerals, including natural fluoride. The phenomenon was written about in newspapers and magazines around the world.

Deaf Smith County itself was named for one of the heroes of the Texas Revolution, Erastus "Deaf" Smith. Smith was born in New York but his family moved to Mississippi and later Texas, where he made his home in 1821. He moved around trying to improve his health but never overcame his deafness. Smith married a Mexican woman and was neutral when the Texans started their move toward independence from Mexico, but his neutrality ended over a personal dispute with the Mexicans. Smith went to San Antonio to visit his family but was refused admittance and, as a result, decided to join the Texans. He was well known as a scout and his services were accepted when he volunteered. Smith served loyally throughout the battles for independence and is considered by some as a little-known hero of the Texas Revolution.

Before Texas won its independence from Mexico in 1836, the Nueces River was considered the border between the two lands. The Texans, dictating the peace terms to Mexican dictator General Santa Anna, put the border at the Rio Grande River. When he balked, they showed him a hangman's rope and he agreed. This was never accepted by the Mexican government, however, which led to the Mexican-American War of 1846. The border was not agreed upon until Mexico signed the treaty of Guadalupe Hidalgo in 1848.

☆

The worst U.S. natural disaster occurred in Texas—the Great Storm of 1900 in Galveston. By 4 o'clock the afternoon of September 8, Galveston had suffered pounding rain for four days and was under two feet of standing water. In some areas water was five feet deep. Four hours later, winds peaked at 120 mph and a huge wave of water pushed through the island town, smashing buildings and snapping trees. Six thousand people drowned; some historians put the number at eight thousand. After the storm, the town's population had been reduced by one-third, counting not only the dead and missing, but the seven thousand who moved out of Galveston and never returned.

☆

An example of Texas' diversified geographical makeup and resources is the story of the "Great Pearl Rush" of 1909-11. When very valuable pearls were discovered in Caddo Lake in East Texas, many came with their families to camp on the banks of the lake and search for freshwater mussels containing the pearls. Although this might seem a strange phenomenon for a place like Texas, it was not an isolated incidence, as pearls of various hues have been found in the Concho River as well.

True to its "bigger and better" boast, Texas has a historical marker taller than the Washington Monument and the Statue of Liberty. It is the San Jacinto Monument, located at the San Jacinto Battleground near Houston. At 570 feet, it is confirmed by the 1933 *Guinness Book of Records* to be the world's tallest column monument.

Texans are not strangers to patriotism, and this is vividly pointed out in Stonewall County where the town of Old Glory is located. The original name of the town was New Brandenburg, but anti-German sentiment during World War I was so strong that the citizens changed the name of their town to something they deemed more patriotic; hence, Old Glory.

Much has been said and written about the wisdom of the early American Indian culture. Their healing practices and methods have been particularly lauded and passed down by early settlers in Texas. The Indians' primitive understanding of healing properties of plants was not their only wisdom about our soil, as demonstrated by their agricultural practices. According to the *Handbook of Texas*, "The gardening tribes of Indians had pretty well discovered the western limits of dependable production under primitive methods when Europeans appeared on the scene. Their garden villages at Waco, on Village Creek between Dallas and Fort Worth, and on the Red River in Montague County (San Teadora of Spanish records) marked the boundary where corn planting ceased and a hunting life began. The border coincides rather closely with the Western Cross Timbers and the thirty-inch rainfall line. The East Texas Indians prepared their fields for maize, beans, and squash by burning off the ground. Seeds were planted with a sharp stick, and the freshly burned ground required little cultivation. The shoulder blade of a deer or buffalo served as a hoe for such digging or weed-killing as was done. When a plot of ground became unproductive or weed-infested, a new place was planted, permitting nature to restore the fertility of the depleted plot by the accumulation of plant residues."

The ghost town of Terlingua has made a name for itself as the "chili cookoff capital of the world." This newly found "resource" has almost brought the once-bustling mining town back into the classification of living. Terlingua was established as a silver mine; however, it did not develop into a community until large deposits of quicksilver or mercury were discovered and profitably mined. When the mining ceased, the town died.

One West Texas town featured the lowly tumbleweed as its Christmas decoration. Anson, located at the center of Jones County, still celebrates its "Cowboy Christmas Ball." Since it began in 1885, cowpokes and tenderfoots alike have traveled from all over Texas to attend the event. Tumbleweed had been used for holiday decoration until recent years when modern times caught up with tradition and authorities declared the weed a fire hazard and banned its use.

The last Civil War battle fought in Texas was near Brownsville on May 13, 1865. In the battle, Confederate General John S. Ford defeated 800 Union troops.

More species of bats live in Texas than any other part of the United States, but one would be surprised to learn where, geographically and specifically, they live. An estimated 1.5 million Mexican free-tailed bats dwell under the Congress Avenue bridge in Austin.

One Texas town was a shipping port second only to Galveston, and it wasn't even located on the coast! The quaint and very picturesque town of Jefferson, on Caddo Lake in East Texas, was at one time known as the "Riverport to the Southwest." By using a chain of lakes and bayous to the Red River, flat-bottomed steamboats could travel up the river to Jefferson and then to Shreveport, enabling the shipping and receipt of goods without overland transport. One interesting footnote must be added when talking about this history-rich town. Jay Gould, the noted financier known as the "Wizard of Wall Street," offered to build a railroad through Jefferson. The city fathers voted, however, not to furnish right-of-ways or subsidize Gould's railway in any way. An angry Gould, upon leaving town, wrote the following "curse" in the hotel registry: "Grass will grow in your streets and bats will roost in your belfries," a prediction that without the railroad, the decline of Jefferson was certain. Subsequent events which resulted in a change of available waterways made the town inaccessible to shipping, which assured Jefferson's decline and made Gould's curse a reality. Visitors there today will find grass growing in some of the lightly traveled streets, although it is a magnificent old town with many original buildings and homes—some of which are open for tours or are bed-and-breakfasts. There are also some nice shops, and Jay Gould's private railroad car is on display for tours. But one must admit it is not the center of commerce it was when Jay Gould put his curse on it.

One of the most interesting bits of geographic trivia involves the naming of the Brazos River. A very poignant legend, accepted by most historians as fact, involves the explorer Francisco de Coronado, who in 1716 with his expedition party wandered through Texas for days without water and would have died had a band of Indians not led them to a stream. Upon finding the water, a padre accompanying the expedition exclaimed, "los brazos de dios!" which means "the arms of God!" Thus the life-saving body of water became the Brazos.

Just as Houston's Astrodome changed the playing of certain sports in Texas, and to some degree across the nation, another kind of dome was instrumental in changing the entire economy of Texas, as well as its image. Created eons ago, the geological formations called salt domes, found particularly along the Gulf Coast plains, were the basis for Texas' petroleum industry. The domes trapped and housed the oil and natural gas that gave Texas some of its most productive fields and were responsible for driving the speculators and drillers into oil exploration throughout Texas. One such salt dome produced the fabulous Lucas gusher known as Spindletop, which came in near Beaumont on January

10, 1901. The Spindletop gusher was so powerful that before it was capped it erupted more than 75,000 barrels a day for six to nine days. Long before Europeans arrived on the oil-rich Texas soil, Indians touted the oil as having medicinal qualities.

☆

Although the actual facts elude us, legends abound as to how the old town of Dime Box got its name. One legend involves a wooden ferry across the river near where the town was established. A rope was stretched across the river at the boat site so that crossers could pull themselves across in the boat, and nailed to a tree near the crossing was a metal box. A sign on the tree instructed the user to "deposit a dime in the box." The community grew up around this "honor system" ferry and was named Dime Box. Another story maintains that the residents of a rural community at the site prevailed upon the postmaster to shop for them when he was in town, bringing their purchases with the next mail delivery. The accommodating postmaster put up a metal box in the mercantile store with instructions that anyone wishing him to do errands for them should put a dime in the box.

Texas' immense size is best illustrated by the fact that the Panhandle city of Dalhart is closer to the capitals of four other states (New Mexico, Oklahoma, Kansas, and Colorado) than it is to the Texas capital in Austin. Mileages are as follows: Dalhart to Austin, 537; Dalhart to Santa Fe, N.M., 327; Dalhart to Oklahoma City, 309; Dalhart to Denver, Colorado, 471; Dalhart to Topeka, Kansas, 489.

Not all Texas towns can boast pretentious or romantic namesakes. Such is the case of Clyde, located in the West Texas county of Callahan, which sprang up around the construction of the Texas & Pacific Railroad in 1881. The town was named for Robert Clyde, a camp boss of a railroad construction gang. Why Clyde was so honored and immortalized on the state maps of Texas has eluded present-day records. But the town name proves that one does not have to be a great hero or statesman to find a place in the history books!

According to the *Handbook of Texas*, the original name of El Paso was Coon's Rancho, or Franklin, as it was sometimes called. Franklin Coons or Coontz, was a Santa Fe trader who established a store on the Rio Grande in the area of present-day El Paso sometime prior to 1848. Three companies of United States troops under Benjamin Beale were stationed at the Rancho in 1849. Coons became postmaster in 1850 and the settlement was officially named Franklin. With the incorporation of Moffinsville, Hart's Mill, and Concordia, the conglomerate became El Paso.

The first suspension bridge in Texas was built across the Brazos River at Waco in 1870. This was thirteen years before the Brooklyn Bridge in New York was built. At the time it was the only span across the Brazos.

There are three Indian reservations in existence in Texas. They are the Alabama-Coushatta, located at Livingston, Polk County; the Tigua, in El Paso County; and the Kickapoo, south of Eagle Pass.

The naming of one Texas river was influenced by the pecan. According to Texas history, the Spaniards discovered and named the Nueces River, which in Spanish means "river of nuts."

One of Texas' most publicized rivers was named for the raw material used by the Indians in the making of weapons and tools. President Lyndon Johnson's beloved Pedernales River was so named because of the large amount of flint rock found there. The Spanish word for flint, or arrowhead, is *pedernal*.

The crossing of the Nueces River by United States troops led by General Zachary Taylor, and the crossing of the Rio Grande by Mexican troops, which resulted in the death of several Americans in a skirmish near Brownsville on April 25, 1846, inaugurated the Mexican-American War. Two other battles were fought on what is now Texas soil. During the war, Governor James Pinkney Henderson left his office to serve as a major general of volunteers. The war ended February 2, 1848, with the signing of the Treaty of Guadalupe Hidalgo. As a result, Mexico, for the first time, renounced any claims to Texas and accepted the Rio Grande as the boundary between the United States and Mexico.

The oldest settlements in Texas are the missions and pueblos of Ysleta and Socorro, located near present-day El Paso. They were established in 1862 in Mexico across the Rio Grande from El Paso and remained in Mexico until the flooding of the Rio Grande in the early nineteenth century moved them to the Texas side of the international boundary set by the treaty ending the Mexican-American War. The United States obtained these pueblos through a "land grab" assisted by Mother Nature.

Stamford, Texas, has its own unique claim to recognition, especially to rodeo lovers across the country. The Texas Cowboy Reunion, known to many simply as the Stamford Rodeo, is much more than just a western entertainment event. The Texas Cowboy Reunion, a state-chartered nonprofit institution, held its first rodeo at Stamford on June 18, 1930. The reunion was organized to preserve the history and customs of the old-time Texas cowboy. It features a three-day celebration and is attended by cowmen and visitors from many places in the United States.

One Texas community was named for a story in a magazine. Capitola, in Mason County fifteen miles west of Mason on the old Menard Road, was sparsely settled in 1894. When a post office was established, Mrs. Sarah E. Jenkins was appointed postmistress. She named Capitola for a continued story she was reading at the time the Postal Service granted the request for a post office. The town went out of existence when the road was changed.

The lowest pass through the Rocky Mountains is in Texas. The pass, earlier known by its Spanish name, "El Paso Del Norte," is guarded by the present city of El Paso.

☆

The so-called "Frying-pan Ranch" was located in today's Potter County in the Panhandle. It was built as a model ranch to demonstrate the effectiveness of the newly marketed barbed wire. Its cattle brand was in the shape of a panhandle, and as a result, cowboys on the ranch renamed it "Frying-pan Ranch."

Among those Texas cities having an unsuitable name is Beaumont, founded in 1835 when its first reputed Anglo settler, Noah Tevis, sold fifty acres of land to the Thomas Huling Company through its agent, Henry Millard. A townsite was laid out and named Beaumont, which means in French, "beautiful mountain." Some say Millard named the city for a relative, while others say it was named for a slight elevation southeast of the city. The latter seems preposterous, since the highest elevation in Beaumont, located on the Gulf Coast, is thirty-six feet above sea level.

Some Texas town names reflect the state's violent history. Such is the case with Babyhead Mountain in Llano County. This mountain was so named in 1850 when settlers discovered that raiding Comanche Indians had captured a white baby and put its head on a pole on the mountain.

Although many people visit Big Bend National Park each year, few are aware that the mountains which form its eastern boundary are known locally as the "dead horse" mountains. Generally called the Sierra del Carmens, they are known in Brewster County as Caballo Muerta, dead horse in Spanish. The name came from an 1879 incident involving a surveying party from Presidio led by Captain Charles Nevill of the Texas Rangers. Under attack by Indians, the party killed their own horses rather than let them fall into the hands of the Indians.

Texas is fortunate enough to boast of having its own
Bunker Hill. The Texas town of the same name is in
Jasper County and was named for the famed Revolu-
tionary War battle by early settlers from Massachusetts.

One community in Polk County was named in honor of
two of the town's benefactresses. Marianna, Texas
(originally Drew's Landing) was established in southern
Polk County in 1838 by Monroe Drew, who was an
Indian trader dealing with the Alabama-Couchatta. A
post office was established in 1871 and given the name
Marianna in honor of Mary and Annie Goodrich, who
donated an organ to the town's church.

What's in a name? Sometimes a lot more than we think.
Although the records reflect the Rio Grande Valley town
of Mercedes was named for Mercedes Diaz, wife of
Mexican President Porfirio Diaz, there may be more to
the name than even the town's residents know. The
original name of the community was Lonsboro, after Lon
C. Hill, an agent and promoter. In 1905 the American
Land and Irrigation Company changed the name, which
may be more appropriate for other reasons. It is said that
in the 1750s, the Spanish Crown gave generous land
grants called "merceds" (meaning king's mercy) along the
Rio Grande to Spaniards of "reliability," meaning
wealthy ranchers. Mercedes was settled by Mexican
ranchers in the late 1770s on early land grants.

The first site in Texas to be named is thought to be
Anaqua, located on the San Antonio River in southern

Victoria County. It was described by Cabeza de Vaca as the habitat of the depraved tribe of Anaqua Indians. Carlos de Garza built a ranch and a chapel at the site around 1820. Anglo-American settlers came after 1836, and Anaqua continued to be a thriving settlement until 1905, when the Missouri-Pacific Railroad laid tracks five miles to the east and drew away many settlers.

Not only is the Brazos River the longest river wholly in Texas, it has great historical significance. The river was well known to Spanish explorers and missionaries, who told of Indians living along its banks; however, the first permanent settlements on the river were established by Anglo-Americans. John McFarland, a member of the "Old Three Hundred," founded San Felipe de Austin at the Atascosito crossing of the Brazos. The town became the colonial capital of Texas. The river also acquired further significance at Columbia and Washington-on-the-Brazos, the sites of the first two seats of government of the Republic. And the first bloody battle for Texas independence took place along the Brazos at Velasco.

Texas has its share of towns that are misnomers. Here are a few examples:

Big Lake, located in southern Reagan County, according to historians, has no big lake. It is named so because of a large depression two miles south of town which briefly becomes a lake in wet seasons, remaining filled for two or three days and then suddenly draining. The phenomenon is unexplained except for the theory that the water drains into an underground river.

Sweetwater, in north-central Nolan County, was founded on Sweetwater Creek, but residents and anyone else familiar with the area knows that the water there is anything but sweet!

Mobeetie, in Tyler County, was originally named Sweetwater. When the townspeople applied for a post office in 1879 they had to select a new name because there was already another Sweetwater. A tongue-in-cheek story goes that a local Indian offered his name, Mobeetie, which was later discovered to mean "buffalo chip." However, the *Handbook of Texas* tells us that mobeetie is the Indian word for sweet water.

Iraan, though an oil town, has no connection with the Middle East country similarly named. Located five miles west of the Pecos River in Pecos County, Iraan became a town in 1928 when oil was discovered on a large ranch owned by Ira G. Yates. The name was chosen in a contest, the prize for which was a choice town lot. Iraan is a combination of Ira and Ann Yates' names.

Iatan, located on the Texas and Pacific Railroad in Mitchell County, has a name which locals, according to Hub Hagler, attribute to a child with a lisp. Hub says that when schoolchildren were asked if they could suggest a name for the town, the boy with a lisp held up his hand and said "I uh tan." The name Iatan stuck!

Texas has some unusual monuments:

The equestrian statue of Sam Houston on north Main Street in Houston has geographical significance. Sam Houston is posed on his horse so that his arm points in the general direction of the battlefield where he won his greatest victory for Texas—San Jacinto.

Although not a historical monument in the strictest sense, the statue of William Marsh Rice, founder of Rice University in Houston, sits atop the philanthropist's remains. Rice's ashes are buried under his statue on the university campus.

Texas' largest monument is not even made of stone! The U.S. Navy battleship USS *Texas* served the country in two world wars, including as a flagship for Admiral Ernest J. King, Commander of the Atlantic fleet in WW II. At the end of the war, beyond her age of retirement, the "Mighty T" was given to the state of Texas. A commission was established to pay for towing the ship to Texas and providing a permanent berth. The vessel was placed in the Houston Ship Channel near the San Jacinto Monument.

The productive and lush greenbelt that we call the Rio Grande Valley was not always such a paradise. It is said that prior to the early 1900s when the railroad brought midwestern farmers who recognized its agricultural potential, only cactus and retama, a thorny shrub, grew in the sandy soil there.

Enchanted Rock is a rare state treasure in that it is not only steeped in history, legend, and lore, but is in its original condition! Located in northeastern Gillespie County at the county line south of the town of Llano, the bald, oval-shaped granite dome rises from the wildflowered countryside to a height of 1,800 feet above sea level. From its summit in the fall of 1841 Captain John Coffee (Jack) Hays, surrounded by Comanche Indians who cut him off from his Ranger company, deflected the entire band and inflicted upon them such heavy losses that they fled. Other Indian legends and lore about this much-visited Texas landmark make it a truly enchanting place to visit. The Comanche Indians gave the rock its name because they believed it was haunted. Their beliefs are based on the sounds often heard at the site, especially at night. It is believed that the mysterious sounds are caused by the contracting of stones in the cool of the night, especially after a hot day. The Indians credited the rock with having a spirit and offered it sacrifices, hoping for successful raids on white settlements. According to Indian lore, an Indian chief was condemned to wander over the rock to appease the gods. When thinking of that, you may be compelled to look over your shoulder if you visit the rock at dusk!

Although usually the term "free state" refers to an independent country, or an area within a country with an independent government, this was not the case in Texas. Van Zandt County was created in 1848 out of Henderson County and given the name "Free State of Van Zandt." One story explaining this says that when the county was created, the old county retained all its debts, while Van Zandt was free of debt. It was therefore a "free state."

The "daddy of all Texas rivers," the Rio Grande, has been known at different times and various places along its course as "Rio del Norte," "Rio San Buenoventura," "Rio Turbio," and "Rio Bravo." The name Rio Grande was given the stream by explorer Juan de Oñate, who arrived at its banks near today's El Paso in 1598. From source to mouth, the river drops 12,000 feet to sea level. The length of the river depends on the method of measurement and varies yearly as its course changes; the latest Water Commission figure is 1,896 miles. Again depending on the method of measurement, the Rio Grande is the fourth or fifth longest river in North America and is Texas' longest river. It irrigates a broad valley of central New Mexico dating from the 1600s, the oldest irrigated area in the United States. Through the Big Bend the Rio Grande flows through three successive canyons—Santa Elena, Mariscal, and Boquillas. The river drains over 40,000 square miles of Texas.

Bon Ami, in Jasper County, may very well be a clean place to live, but it was not named for the well-known scouring powder. Its name honors a Louisiana town by the same name. Clean or not, the town should be friendly: its name, in French, means "good friend."

The first immigrants to Ector County found wide rolling plains covered with mesquite and underbrush. Because of their resemblance to the steppes of Russia, an official of the newly built Texas and Pacific Railroad named the first settlement Odessa.

According to archaeologists, the site of one of the oldest areas of human habitation in North America is near Lubbock, Texas. Discovered in 1936, the site dates back to the Clovis period some 12,000 years ago. The site is located at Yellow House Draw in northeastern Lubbock County. The draw supposedly was named for Indian cave dwellings in the yellowish bluffs at Yellow House Lake.

The original Spanish name was "Laguna de las Casas Amarillas."

Carrollton, Texas, in Dallas County was established in 1872 as a stop on the Katy Railroad. Much of the town was comprised of a post office and businesses moved there from Trinity Mills when the M.K.&T. Railroad was built in 1872. Carrollton was known locally as "the town you went over, not through" because Highway 77 which went from Dallas to Denton had a high bridge which went over much of the town.

Vying with Loving County for the title of least populated, Winkler County is located on the southern edge of Texas' high plains. The lack of population kept the county joined to Reeves County until 1910, until enough people lived there to justify county organization. The first schools opened and the first election was held, with forty-three votes cast. The county commissioner's court met; the voters had selected the Kermit Hotel for the courthouse and thus Kermit became the county seat. (Incidentally, Kermit was the only town in Winkler County.) Early records of Winkler County deal with money appropriations for "grubbing out bear-grass from the courthouse yard, the purchase of water tanks and troughs, and bounties paid for dead rabbits, wolves, and wildcats." In 1916 a drought began that lasted until 1922 and broke many a rancher, causing most to move away. In 1920 the county's population was eighty-one, of whom only nineteen were voters. By 1926 all the county officials lived outside the county. Newcomers were not eligible to vote, and at that time there were only six legal voters in the county!

☆

Henry Doering could have never foreseen that the tin-sided mercantile building he built over 100 years ago in the Williamson County farming community near Georgetown would ring with the yodeling and singing of another German immigrant who, with his chef partner, turned it into a German restaurant of statewide acclaim. Doering, who immigrated to the county in 1882, bought many acres of land in the area and used it to attract his fellow countrymen to Texas. Doering built the store and a bank, which, along with two Lutheran churches, formed the town of Walburg, named after Doering's birthplace in Germany. German-speaking residents can still be found in the area today.

Old red-brick bank building built in 1913 in Walburg.

This tin-sided mercantile building built by Henry Doering in 1882 is now a popular German restaurant.

Although its name seems inviting enough, Loving County, located on the south plains of West Texas, has always been sparsely populated. Only six farms existed there in 1945, in an area of 647 square miles. Loving County was created from Tom Green County in 1887, and by 1890 its population was a whopping three. By 1900 there were only thirty-two inhabitants. Oil was discovered in 1925, and the population was reported at 195 in 1930. The county was organized in 1893 and was the last Texas county to be organized; the county government was organized in 1931 with Mentone as the county seat. There are no railroads across the area, and less than four miles of highways lead from the Pecos to Mentone. Population was 227 in 1950, making Loving the least populous of all Texas counties.

One might assume that the town of Dublin in Erath County was named after the famous city in Ireland. But though logical, that would be a wrong assumption. Dublin, founded in 1854 and named in 1860, was originally "Doublin," derived from the cry "double in," a warning that an Indian raid was imminent.

☆

Nestled in the Hill Country county of Bandera is a beautiful oddity. Lost Maples State Park is home to bigtooth maple trees that are "lost" because they are hundreds of miles south of usual maple habitat. Left over from an earlier, colder climate, the stand of maples still clings hard-headedly to the hills of southwest Texas, amid other vegetation long since changed to suit the warmer climate created when the last ice age ended.

☆

The Sad Monkey Railroad is a two-mile loop of miniature railroad that runs through Palo Duro Canyon State Park, twelve miles east of Canyon, Texas, on Ranch Road 217. The railroad is named for one of the canyon's many unusual rock formations.

The town of Preston, in northern Grayson County, originated with the establishment of Holland Coffee's Trading House on the Red River in 1837. An important shipping point during Texas' Republic days, Preston was also the site of Coffee's impressive two-story mansion,

Glen Eden. The home stood long after its original inhabitants were gone and might have still been there, but the creation of Lake Texoma submerged the site of old Preston, and the structure was dismantled.

The Comal River rises from a number of large springs in the northwestern part of New Braunfels in Comal County and flows southeast into the Guadalupe River. The name Comal comes from a Spanish word for a flat earthernware pan used to cook maize cakes. The numerous small, flat islands in the river reminded early Spaniards of the pans. The two-and-a-half mile river is the shortest in Texas, and according to the *Handbook of Texas*, "It is said to be the shortest river carrying a large body of water in the United States."

A hand-drawn map of early Denton County settlements included an unusual land formation on the North Texas blackland prairie. Identified on the map as Pilot Knob, it was noteworthy not only because of its topography but also because of its interest to aficionados of Texas outlaws. The 900-foot knob of earth located about four miles from the city of Denton was supposedly a hangout for stage, train, and bank robber Sam Bass. Wayne Gard, in his biography of Sam Bass, alluded to Bass's relationship with Pilot Knob. In one reference Gard reported that Bass, while on the run from a posse, stopped at a farm at Pilot Knob to buy provisions. He also indicated that Bass used the high point on the North Texas prairie as a lookout. The person who drew the map also referred to the Knob as a "rendezvous point for Sam Bass," and he and his gang supposedly hid in a cave there. Based on facts pointed out in Robert Nash's book *Badmen and Blood-letters*, Bass and his gang may have been hiding out at the Knob when they planned their ill-fated attempt at robbing the bank at Round Rock near Austin, Texas, in which Bass was mortally wounded on July 19, 1878.

The Cross Timbers of Texas are two long, narrow strips of forest region extending parallel to each other from Oklahoma southward to central Texas, according to the *Handbook of Texas*. The wooded areas, known as the Eastern or Lower Cross Timbers and the Western or Upper Cross Timbers, contrast sharply with the surrounding prairie land. The Eastern or Lower Cross Timbers extend through the eastern parts of Denton, Tarrant, and Johnson Counties and is probably the region referred to by early settlers near present-day Grapevine, Texas. The church history of Lonesome Dove Baptist Church, established in 1846, reports that "Many of the first members lived in the edge of Cross Timbers." The original minutes of the church identifies their location as Cross Timbers.

Fort Spunky, Texas, in southeastern Hood County, was originally Barnardville, named after Barnard's Trading House in 1847. It earned its current name after several fights broke out while the town was in the process of getting its post office.

★

The dungeon-like jail of Fort Davis, one-time county seat of Presidio County, was underneath the adobe court house. Known as the "bat cave," its entrance was a trap door and ladder in the floor of the sheriff's office.

According to the minutes of the Commissioner's Court, it was outfitted with five iron cages and a scaffold. Referring to the move to the new county seat, the court minutes indicate that "all records, books, and furniture except five iron cages and a scaffold in the jail have been moved to Marfa." The old "bat cave" courthouse was replaced on the same site with a modern concrete and stone structure in 1911.

Texas has two cities that are located in two states. Texhoma, in northeastern Sherman County on the Texas-Oklahoma border, was established in 1900 and is Texas' northernmost city. Its banks, post office, and much of its business district are on the Oklahoma side. Texarkana, in Bowie County, straddles the Texas-Arkansas state line. While commercially one city, Texarkana has two sets of councilmen and city officials. There is a cooperative arrangement for joint operation of the fire department and other services. The federal building has the distinction of being the only building of its kind situated in two states, and the post office is the only one in the nation serving two states. The address: Texarkana USA 75502. A marker in front of the building is a favorite spot for pictures, as it enables one to be photographed in two states at once.

Roosevelt, Texas, was named for Theodore Roosevelt. Located in Kimble County on Interstate 10, it has no north-south access, as there is no crossroad and one enters and leaves town traveling east or west. A traffic sign in the town says "East with an arrow and West with an arrow." The town consists primarily of a store and a post office.

A region composed of five communities—Millheim in Austin County, Latium in Washington County, Sisterdale and Tusculum in Kendall County, and Bettina in Llano County—was settled in the 1840s by highly educated Germans. Literature seemed to be the catalyst that bonded the settlements, and it is written that regular debates were held in Latin. Incidentally, Latium was the name of the Latin-speaking region in Italy which included Rome.

☆

The picturesque Hill Country town of Fredericksburg has a built-in friendly greeting for visitors. The first letters of the street names going east from the Vereins Kirche (church) spell "All Welcome." Those going west spell "Come Back." Locals explain that in the town's early days a lot of people came through Fredericksburg from the East on their way out West. So they got their welcome from the east and an invitation to return as they departed westward.

☆

The Alibates Flint Quarries in the Texas Panhandle, near the Canadian River, have been exploited by man for at least 12,000 years, according to the *Handbook of Texas*. Anthropologists who visited the site in 1930 recognized the quarry as the source of flint for weapon points and implements for some of the first men on the North American continent. After an appeal in 1962 for recognition, a law put into effect in 1965 established the quarry and the Panhandle pueblo culture a national monument. The name Alibates came from the unintentional corruption of the name of a young cowboy who lived in a line camp at the quarry site in the late 1800s, Allie Bates.

The town of Hazel Dell in Comanche County might have been another Tombstone, Arizona, as it was reputed to be the capital of lawlessness in Comanche County. The town's physician was said to have been an expert on gunshot wounds. Nothing remains of the town today except a few farm houses and a "boot hill" reputation.

Fort Davis, located in the Davis Mountains of far West Texas, was established in 1854 and gained distinction by serving as the county seat of two counties. From 1875 to 1885 it was the county seat of Presidio; after Jeff Davis County was created, Fort Davis became county seat of the newer county.

Electra, in Wichita County about ten miles south of the Red River, has had two other names: Beaver and Waggoner. The first settlement followed the building of the Fort Worth and Denver Railroad through the area in 1885. The first post office, secured in 1889, was named Beaver, and the settlement was a trading post for Chief Quanah Parker and his Comanche comrades. Daniel Waggoner and his son, W.T. Waggoner, had moved their herds from Wise County westward in 1878 and established headquarters on the Red River north of the present location of Electra. To prevent clashes between cattlemen and farmers because of damage done by the herds driven to shipping points, Waggoner induced the railroad to build switch tracks and loading pens at Beaver in 1910. When the first depot was built, it was designated Waggoner. The town's citizens petitioned in 1902 to have the town named Electra to honor Electra Waggoner, daughter of W.T. Waggoner.

When the Fort Worth and Denver Railroad was constructed across the Panhandle county of Potter in 1887, a construction crew camped on the property of Jess Jenkins, where a collection of buffalo hide huts and tents called "Ragtown" became the nucleus of present-day Amarillo. Henry B. Sanborn laid out a townsite one mile southeast of Ragtown near Amarillo Lake, named by Mexican herders because of the yellow color of the banks of the lake. The county seat remained Ragtown until 1893.

Galveston Island was often called "Snake Island" (Isle de Calabras) by the Spaniards. The Spanish navigator Jose de Evia made a survey of the island, bay, and harbor in 1785 and named the bay for Bernard de Galvez, Viceroy of Mexico.

During the 1950s Texas was the nation's leading spinach-producing state. Production was centered in the "winter garden" area of South Texas. At the time, 16,000 acres yielded 2,062,000 bushels valued at $3,608,000. A statue of the cartoon character Popeye was erected at Crystal City, the site of one of the world's largest spinach canneries.

The Big Thicket town of Grayburg was established in 1805 by the Thompson-Ford Lumber Company, which built a lumber mill there. All the buildings were painted gray. Dr. F.L. Thompson, the company physician, suggested the town's name.

The backward (spelled) town of Saxet, Texas, was a farming and cattle-raising community in Shelby County and a shipping point on the Santa Fe Railroad. When the rail spur was removed, Saxet became a ghost town.

The town of Tell, in Childress County, was originally named "Tell Tale Flats," so named because of the propensity of its residents to reveal unsolicited information to the local grand jury. The post office department shortened the name to Tell.

Lonesome Dove, Texas, or the Missouri Colony as it was called, is much more than just the namesake of Larry McMurtry's Pulitzer-prize-winning novel and the TV miniseries it spawned. The real Lonesome Dove, with its blacksmith shop, school, church, and restaurant with a Woodmen of the World hall upstairs, existed on the edge of the Cross Timbers. Many of the settlement's residents moved to nearby Grapevine when the railroad came through there. Today the community site near Dallas-Fort Worth International Airport is dotted with high-priced homes separated by an occasional old home and the bustling shopping centers serving the new inhabitants. The one remaining recognizable remnant of the much publicized fictional town is the red brick Lonesome Dove Baptist Church and its adjoining cemetery, both carved out of a grove of age-old trees which were once part of the Cross Timbers. The church

was established in 1846 by a group of settlers from Platte
County, Missouri, who came to Texas by ox-drawn
wagons and formed the Missouri Colony. Although more
than one version exists as to how the church, and thus
the community, got its name, the one most accepted and
most logical is that at the time of its establishment the
Lonesome Dove Baptist Church was the first church in
Tarrant County and the only Protestant church between
the Trinity River and the Pacific coast. Metaphorically
speaking, Christ (the dove) was understandably a
lonesome figure. It was also said that the church's
committee selecting a name heard the cooing of a
mourning dove during their meeting. This, they reported,
sounded very lonesome and they thought their selection
of a name very fitting. Being so far out on the western
frontier, the area at the time was not lacking a "shoot-em
up" atmosphere; church records reveal that the original
wooden structure was burned by unfriendly Indians who
were killed after being caught. Another historical event in

Lonesome Dove's past was when the church's first clerk was gored by a bull buffalo. He had the dubious honor of being Tarrant County's first surgery patient. The Lonesome Dove cemetery is the resting place of some of Tarrant County's first elected officials after the county's organization in 1850. Also reflecting the dangers of this time on the Texas prairie is the church's report that the walls at the back of the building were often lined with members' guns, brought to church in case of sudden Indian attack. Although author McMurtry's fictional Lonesome Dove was exciting, the facts chronicled by past inhabitants of the real community reflect the true pioneer spirit on the North Texas prairie over 150 years ago.

One of Lonesome Dove's early settlers, John Torian, bought this hand-hewn log cabin in 1886. It was moved from the Lonesome Dove community to Liberty Park on Main Street in Grapevine, Texas.

One of San Antonio's buildings sits on an island. The Tower Life Building (Transit Tower Building) constructed in 1939 and for thirty years the tallest building in the city, sits on what once was Bowen's Island in the San Antonio River.

A town in East Texas changed its name to benefit strawberry shippers. Arp, located in Smith County, was originally Strawberry, Texas. According to the *Handbook of Texas*, the name was changed to honor William Arp, a popular newspaper editor, and to aid strawberry shippers who had to label crates by hand. No doubt the shorter name reduced hand-lettering and thus increased the number of crates a shipper could label in a day.

Waco's historic suspension bridge over the Brazos River predates New York's famous Brooklyn Bridge and was constructed by the same builder. Until the late 1860s, the only way across the Brazos at Waco was by ferry or by fording the river when the water was low. Captain Shapley Ross had operated a primitive ferry at Waco since 1849, but the Brazos could be treacherous after a rain and was sometimes impassable for days at a time. Waco business leaders got a charter from the state in 1866 to build a permanent toll bridge over the Brazos. Even with money scarce and interest rates high during Reconstruction, the Waco Bridge Company sold all its stock, and in mid-1868, the company chose John A. Roebling and Son of Trenton, N.J., to design and build a new suspension-type bridge. Roebling utilized the same style and technique he later used on the Brooklyn Bridge, which opened in 1883. Civil engineer Thomas M. Griffith, a Roebling employee who had worked with similar bridges, was the actual designer and construction supervisor. Work began in September of 1868. At the time, Waco had no machine shops or any artisans with the skills to build a bridge of this magnitude, and the nearest railroad was 100 miles away. The woven wire cables and other components were shipped to Galveston by steamer, transferred by rail to Bryan, then taken by ox wagons on a rutted, dusty road to Waco. Construction began with the excavation for the footings of the twin double towers that would anchor the span. The towers, which required 2.7 million locally produced bricks to construct, were topped with crenelated ornamentation resembling a medieval castle. Workmen carried wires across the river to form the massive cables that would support the wooden roadway. The span was completed in late December 1869, and the first tolls were collected on January 1, 1870. The $141,000 structure—the first bridge across the Brazos—was dedicated five days later. The main span was wide enough for two stagecoaches to pass each other, and it was 475 feet long.

Of all of Austin's landmarks, few have received as much publicity as the Treaty Oak. The famous tree is a 500-year-old live oak with a branch spread of 110 feet. It stands on property on Baylor Street that was acquired by the City of Austin in 1937. The tree was a landmark and popular picnic spot for citizens of Austin before the city engulfed it in the 1880s. The name comes from a local story that Stephen F. Austin signed a treaty with the Indians under its branches, but there is little foundation for this belief. The tree received nationwide attention in recent years when someone tried to kill it by poisoning it. There was much press coverage of its illness and the efforts to save it. The person attempting to kill the old landmark was convicted and sent to jail. The tree seems to be, at the time of this writing, out of danger. Its dead branches were pruned out and sliced into wafers to be sold with certificates of authenticity and the proceeds used to plant other oaks as a living memorial to the famous old landmark.

Mark Wieland, the person in charge of marketing the Treaty Oak, says one proposal would move the marker at the park, erect a new stone monument, and build a display showing the historic tree's past. (photo reprinted with permission of the *Dallas Morning News*)

Before the San Antonio River was included in a federally funded beautification program which resulted in today's Paseo del Rio, or River Walk, some of the city's businessmen wanted to convert the downtown section of the river into a sewer and build a street on top of it.

According to the *Handbook of Texas*, early San Antonio consisted of two towns. The apparently more affluent, aristocratic Canary Islanders lived on one side of the San Antonio River after 1731, separated from La Villita or "little village," which was originally an Indian village. The first huts were erected in La Villita in about 1722. Soldiers attached to the San Antonio de Bexar Presidio lived there. In 1773 La Villita opened to refugees moving to San Antonio from East Texas. Here was the San Antonio of adobe houses with homemade wooden doors. The houses were built of mud and stone with a lean-to made of woven twigs and grass which served as a kitchen. Historians say that the homes were often paid for with livestock.

Taylor County can boast of having a courthouse held together by cannonballs. The old Taylor County courthouse and jail was built in 1879 in Buffalo Gap, which was the county seat prior to 1880, when it was moved to Abilene. The building was built on unstable soil, so the builder hollowed out pockets in the limestone blocks and put in cannonballs hauled from Vicksburg, Mississippi, after the Civil War to lock the blocks together. It is said that after a hundred years, no cracks can be found in the old building, which is now used as a museum.

The "Man who wears the Star" had his beginning at Sour Lake, Texas, in south central Hardin County near the Big Thicket. The town was named for the mineral springs that fed the lake. It was first settled in 1835, but long before white settlers, Indians made use of its mineral springs and the pitch found around the oil seepage along the lake's shore. As early as 1850 it was a health resort with good accommodations for health seekers, including Sam Houston, and continued to be so until the discovery of oil in 1902. The Texas Company, Texaco, had produced about 90,000,000 barrels of oil from its Sour Lake field by 1948.

Austin can lay claim to having the oldest operating public school in Texas. Pease Elementary School was established in 1876, no doubt named for Governor Elisha M. Pease, known as the "education governor." It was Pease who on January 31, 1854, signed the bill setting up the Texas public school system.

The King William District of San Antonio was declared the state's first National Historic District in 1967. The district was the preferred address of San Antonio's large German community in the late 1800s. It was planned by Ernst Altman, who founded the town of Comfort, Texas, in 1854.

The oldest Dr Pepper bottling plant in the world is in Dublin in Erath County. Bill Kloster's 106-year-old plant was opened in 1891 by Sam Houston Prim. The Prim family ran the plant for 100 years before Bill Kloster inherited it in 1991. The drink was invented in about 1885.

It sounds like a tall Texas tale, but the Big Texan Steak Ranch at Amarillo is the real thing. Known to locals and passers-through alike, the restaurant features a 72-ounce steak for $50 (pre-paid) which is free if the customer can finish it in an hour along with the baked potato, shrimp cocktail, and bread that go with it. Carol Barrington, writing in 1995 in *Texas Highways Magazine*, says that since its origin in 1959 some 22,000 beef-eaters have taken the Big Texan challenge. About 3,672 (one in six) have cleaned their plates in the allotted time. The restaurant's founder, R.J. Lee, wanted to prove that Texas cowboys were the biggest eaters and conducted a search for the one who could eat the most. He served the contender one-pound strip steaks until the Texan had eaten four and a half of them (72 ounces). With this as an example he hit upon the idea of offering the 72-ounce challenge.

"Old Cora" is the nickname for the early log cabin in Comanche County that now sits on the present county courthouse lawn in Comanche. "Old Cora" dates back to the town of Cora, which was founded in 1856 and was the county seat of Comanche County from 1856 to 1859. Located ten miles southeast of Comanche, the town was named for Cora Beeman of Bell County. "Old Cora" is considered the oldest existing courthouse in Texas. Some dispute this claim, saying that John Neely Bryan's old log cabin, which is preserved in downtown Dallas, was used as the first courtroom in Dallas. The cabin predates "Old Cora" by fifteen years.

Local Trivia

When the Magnolia Building was the tallest building in Dallas and the flying red horse on top could be seen for miles around, there was a standing riddle which pointed out the neighborly rivalry between Dallas and Fort Worth: "Why are there two horses on top of the Magnolia Building? So that Fort Worth will always know that Dallas is not a one-horse town."

Another bit of Dallas sign trivia involves the Dunkin Donuts sign on top of the downtown store at Elm and Akard Streets. It bore a philosophical piece of advice for the fast-paced Dallas citizens: "As you travel through life, brother, let these words of wisdom be thy goal: Keep your eye on the do-nut and not upon the hole."

The name of one of Dallas' busiest streets was changed due to a controversy. Prior to 1939, Skillman Street was named Charles Lindbergh Street. After moving to Europe in 1935, Lindbergh became acquainted with German field marshal Hermann Goering, head of Nazi Germany's air force. Lindbergh was invited to inspect the air force and afterwards proclaimed it the finest air force in Europe. He was given a decoration by Adolph Hitler.

After he returned to America, he became active in anti-war groups. According to a newspaper article at the time, Lindbergh was called by some "A Nazi agent in the U.S." Public opinion mounted against the American hero, and a movement was started which resulted in the Dallas City Council changing the name of the street to Skillman Street.

☆

A long-running radio show in Dallas featured in its cast "a round man," a "deacon" a "slicker," and a "firecracker." This live show was "The Earlybirds," which broadcast from the studios of WFAA atop the Santa Fe building on Jackson Street. Its master of ceremonies was Jimmy Jefferies, who because of his height and girth was known as "the little round man." The WFAA orchestra was conducted by "Deacon" Wilbur Ard. The program's announcer was Norvel Slater, who because of his baldness was known as "Slicker" Slater. One of the show's regulars was comedian Bob Shelton of Sulphur Springs, whose live-wire antics and personality earned him the reputation of the "Hopkins County firecracker."

☆

Another radio show featuring a band produced a Texas governor. The Lightcrust Doughboys, so named because they were sponsored by the Lightcrust Flour Company, was a "hillbilly" band headed by W. Lee O'Daniel, known throughout Texas as "Pappy" O'Daniel. Because of his popularity among the elderly, for whom he exhibited great sympathy, he ran for the office of governor with a platform based on better old-age pensions and assistance. He won the race handily.

The new Lightcrust Doughboys, led by banjoist Marvin (Smokey) Montgomery in a recent concert. Montgomery joined the original Doughboys in 1935.

The City of Dallas can take pride in claiming to have the first radio station in Texas and the first radio station west of the Mississippi River. WRR-1310 AM began broadcasting in August of 1920. This radio station is still in operation with the call letters WRR FM. WRR can be found at 101.1 FM.

An epidemic of infectious laughter spread through Dallas at Christmastime for several years. Back when all serious shopping was done in downtown Dallas, Sanger Bros., a department store on the corner of Main and Lamar Streets which covered almost a square city block, decorated its Main Street show window one year with a scene depicting Santa and Mrs. Claus in their rocking chairs at home. It was obvious that the culinary skills of

Mrs. Claus were appreciated by both of them. She and the jolly old man were both jelly-bellies. The mechanical animation of the couple was developed to perfection. Added to this homey "hope for a merry Christmas" was a most infectious laugh recording—not this "ho, ho, ho" bit but a really "I'm so tickled" belly laugh—Santa's in his deep but warm voice and Mrs. Claus in a slightly higher grandmotherly voice. This laugh sequence lasted about five minutes and was repeated several times an hour. Passers-by could hear this riotous laughter which was broadcast on speakers. One would have to be made of granite not to find one's own laugh-box turned on by this jovial display of inner fun. The recording had the same effect on the public as a yawn frequently does in a crowded room. Seldom were there fewer than twenty or thirty people standing outside the show window, all convulsing with laughter at the Clauses and at each other. The display was so popular that Sanger Bros. repeated it year after year and it became a tradition until the store closed permanently.

An enterprising woman played an important role in Dallas history. In 1859 Sarah Cockrell chartered the Dallas Iron and Bridge Co., and in 1872 she completed the first iron bridge across the Trinity River. It was a toll bridge until it was purchased by Dallas County in 1882, at which time it became a free bridge.

The "Oak Cliff" section of Dallas was originally called Hord's Ridge.

In 1845 County Judge William H. Hord built this log cabin—the first permanent structure on the west side of the Trinity River in Dallas. In 1887 Oak Cliff developer T. H. Marsalis bought the Hord property in the area then known as "Hord's Ridge." An oak tree stood next to the cabin and was known as the judge's hanging tree, as it was used for that purpose. (photos courtesy *Dallas Times*)

Near the site of the beautiful Bachman Lake in northwest Dallas there was at one time a community of the same name. In 1845 a rural settlement was established on a tributary to the Trinity River just north of present-day Love Field. The community was named for William F. Bachman; the tributary was called Bachman's Branch. The first camp meeting held in Dallas County was held in 1845 at the Missouri-Kansas-Texas railroad crossing of this stream.

☆

Although there are several versions given by historians as to how Fort Worth got the nickname "Panther City," the most accepted one is that in 1875 a Dallas newspaper reported "Fort Worth is such a sleepy town that a panther was spotted dozing unmolested on Main Street!"

☆

Another unverified but interesting morsel of Fort Worth trivia is the story of how the town became the Tarrant County seat. There are those who say that Fort Worth won the election to become the county seat over its nearby rival Birdville by dubious means. According to local lore, Fort Worth stole Birdville's whiskey stash, brought in bogus voters, and then freely dispensed the liquor to influence their votes.

☆

People in Dallas who are familiar with the fashionable Preston Road section of the city would be interested to know that, according to the 1992-93 *Texas Almanac,* "Preston Road was laid out in 1841 following an old Indian trail just after Fort Preston was built on the Red River in present-day Grayson County. It connected the fort to Austin by way of Dallas and Waco."

Early automobile racer and war hero aviator Eddie Rickenbacker came to Dallas in 1908 or 1909 to represent Clinton D. Firestone, whom he had met as a successful car racer, in his automobile company, Firestone Columbus Buggy Company. Rickenbacker frequently demonstrated these early automobiles on Dallas's Chalk Hill to show the prospective buyer how the car could handle inclines. One anecdote told about the aviator says that while he was demonstrating an auto to a customer, the car couldn't pull the hill in first gear. Rickenbacker supposedly turned the negative into a positive by slamming on the brakes and telling the customer, "Just look at those brakes, how they hold on this hill." It is said that the customer bought the car the same day.

The *Dallas Morning News* has a history that parallels that of Texas. The A.H. Belo Corporation, publisher of the *Morning News*, goes back to 1842 and the one-page *Galveston News*, before Texas was even a state! The Belo Corp. is the oldest continuously operating business in Texas. George Bannerman Dealy, who founded the *Morning News* in 1885, was a fifteen-year-old English immigrant when he was hired as an office boy at the *Galveston News*. He was full of enthusiasm and energy and quickly moved up in the company. Working tirelessly, Dealy made his way from office boy to business manager, and then publisher of the *Dallas Morning News*. It was Dealy who chose the then small settlement of Dallas as a site for the sister publication.

Dallas' first local transit system began in 1871. The original system consisted of two mule-drawn streetcars.

The City of Dallas' last horse-drawn fire truck was nicknamed "Old Tige" (an abbreviation for tiger) after former mayor William Lewis Cabell, who acquired the nickname while serving as a general in the Confederate army. Purchased in 1884, the truck was a pumper with a steam boiler which supplied the power for pumping the water. The truck, which was kept in service until 1921, is displayed at the Dallas Firefighter's Museum across from Fair Park at 3801 Parry (at Commerce Street).

Looking "new penny bright," as the day it was bought in 1884 is the city's last horse-drawn fire truck, "Old Tige." The pumper is on exhibit at the Dallas Firefighter's Museum. Also on exhibit is a piece of early Dallas' wooden water main, dug up during recent construction.

Based on a portion of the book *How Fort Worth Became the Texas-Most City*, one is compelled to believe that the American Indians were destined to be totally overcome at the hands of the white man. This book tells us that on December 19, 1875, Comanche Chief Yellow Bear and his nephew, Quanah Parker, checked into the Pickwick Hotel in Fort Worth, which proudly boasted of "artificial gas lights." But this "white man's magic" claimed the life of Chief Yellow Bear. It seems that when the two chiefs turned out the gas lights, they didn't close the valve all the way. When they rolled out their blankets to sleep, Yellow Bear was asphyxiated by the fumes.

Old-timers in Dallas might remember when the Ford Motor Company had a plant on East Grand Avenue, and how each car that rolled off the assembly line proudly bore a decal in the rear window proclaiming "Built in Texas by Texans." This method of manufacturing bragging wasn't a new one, however. In the early 1900s, the Wichita Falls Motor Company, which manufactured trucks, carried the advertisement "Made in Texas for Texas Roads."

Although some say the horned toad or horned frog is really a lizard, it has been identified with Texas almost as much as the armadillo. Fort Worth citizens have no trouble producing a horned frog almost at will, pointing to the campus of Texas Christian University, whose mascot is the horned frog. In 1898 the horned toad was chosen for the name of the yearbook and mascot back when the school was still Add-Ran Christian University and located in Waco. It's said that the reptile population in Waco was so great that they roamed the campus at will. In 1902 the school's name was changed to Texas Christian University. In 1910 the main building burned, and Fort Worth offered the school a fifty-acre campus and $200,000 to move to that city. The university accepted the offer, and after fifteen years in Waco the school moved to Fort Worth.

Two of Dallas' early communities were black settlements whose names have been all but forgotten, although the areas are well-known. Little Egypt, known also as Mission Hill, dates back to Civil War days. The center of this black community was Egypt Chapel Baptist Church, which was sold in 1962. Little Egypt was a thirty-five-acre tract located north of Northwest Highway bounded by Easton Road and Ferndale. Elm Thicket (or Ellum Thicket) was a community of freed slaves located between University Park on the east and Love Field on the west.

If you have ever eaten at the quaint old Stagecoach Inn or shopped the antique stores of historic old Salado off Interstate 35 in northern Bell County, you might have been close to becoming a millionaire with just a little luck and digging. According to a February 1965 edition of the *Dallas Times Herald*, a Dallasite named H. D. McCord and Leo Guerra were searching for a room buried by a landslide. The room supposedly had been first discovered in 1958 by Guerra acting on instructions from an Indian who had since died. Guerra claimed the room, which he had found by navigating a labyrinth of caves, contained 2,000 bars of gold and 600 bars of silver, as well as stacks of coins and a life-size golden bull's head with ruby eyes and other artifacts. Guerra supposedly abandoned the roomful of treasures because of "hunger, fatigue, and fear of survival." He was hospitalized, and after he got out, a rockslide had buried the entrance to the treasure trove.

Rockwall County and its county seat, the town of Rockwall, were named after an outcropping of a subterranean dike or rock wall that can be seen in several places in the county. The wall was discovered in 1852 by Terry Wade as he was digging a well. An article in a 1987 edition of the *Dallas Morning News* says that the wall extends five to forty feet below the ground. Much scientific study of the wall has been made and the findings vary between it being a natural geological formation and the construction of a very early tribe. The way the large stones are so geometrically fitted together lends credence to the latter, but not many can view the formation to test this hypothesis, as the owner of the land where it is exposed refuses to allow public access.

One of Dallas' office buildings is conspicuous by its historical marker. The SEDCO Building located on North Akard Street where former Texas governor Bill Clements had his offices is known as the old Cumberland School. The school was built in 1889 on Cochran and Caruth Streets (now known as Akard Street). This was an elite neighborhood, and many prominent Dallasites attended the school. The neighborhood gradually became largely Hispanic in population and bordered what is known as "Little Mexico." Some of Dallas' early Hispanic immigrants attended the school. The school has been restored with much care, and some of the offices are furnished with period furniture.

The 1889 Cumberland School in Dallas will conjure up many
memories for early Dallasites (many of whom were Dallas' first
Hispanic settlers).

The "high-five" hand gesture in today's slang is a
congratulatory gesture, generally among athletes. But
there was a time in Dallas when the term had more
perilous implications. When the old city hall was located
on the corner of Harwood and Main Streets, the Dallas
city jail was located on the fifth floor. The jail was
irreverently called "High Five," especially among those
who were periodically incarcerated. At that time a
threatening word of caution was "If you don't stop this
or that, you'll end up on High Five!"

One of the best known hospitals in Fort Worth was
named for a former Texas Ranger lawman. John Peter

Smith was born in Owen County, Kentucky, and after graduating from Bethany College in Virginia in 1853 he came to Texas and located in Fort Worth. In 1854 Smith opened a private school. He later became a surveyor and was involved in surveying land in Brazos County. After returning to Fort Worth he studied law and was admitted to the bar in 1860. During the same year he enlisted in the Texas Rangers. Although an anti-secessionist, Smith raised a company of men from Tarrant County and served with them in New Mexico and Louisiana. He came back to Fort Worth and was elected mayor. Known for his interest in the development of Fort Worth, Smith was instrumental in the development of the Fort Worth Stockyards. He died in April of 1901 in St. Louis, Missouri, after he was attacked and robbed while on a business trip.

Although General William Jenkins Worth, for whom the fort and city on the Trinity River was named, did not graduate from West Point, he was commandant at the military academy from 1820 to 1828. Worth, who fought under General Zachary Taylor in the Mexican War, was breveted a brigadier general by President James K. Polk for his services in the Seminole War. The fort, originally known as Camp Worth, was under command of Major Ripley A. Arnold.

The Works Progress Admininstration guide to Dallas points out that what became one of Dallas' most fashionable addresses, Swiss Avenue, was so named because it was originally settled by a group of Swiss immigrants who came to Dallas after Swiss-born Dallas mayor Benjamin Long, a former La Reunion colonist, returned to Zurich in 1870 and persuaded a group of his countrymen to immigrate. Almost three dozen arrived in December of 1870 and built homes along what would become Swiss Avenue.

Highland Park, an incorporated city within Dallas, and Beverly Hills, California, were both planned by landscape designer Wilbur David Cook.

According to the registry of historical buildings in Dallas, the Volk shoe store and company headquarters on Elm Street between Ervay and St. Paul Streets was the first fully air-conditioned building of two or more stories in the nation.

The first manufacturing plant in Dallas was a wagon-making plant opened in 1852 by Maxime Guillot, who had been a wagon-maker at the military post in Fort Worth.

Records indicate that the first black resident of Dallas County was Allen (Al), a blacksmith. He was a slave of John Huitt, who came to Dallas before 1843. Huitt was Dallas' first sheriff, elected in 1846.

Although it is common knowledge that U.S. currency is printed in Washington by the Bureau of Engraving and Printing, few realize that since 1991, some American currency has been printed in the Bureau's printing facility in Fort Worth.

Dallas' first professional baseball team was the Dallas Giants of the Texas League. The team won the league pennant in 1910 at Gaston Park, which at the time was located southwest of what is now Fair Park. Gaston Park was purchased and added to Fair Park and today the site is occupied by the Music Hall.

The first suburban shopping center in Dallas grew up at the Interurban Railway stop at Peak and Bryan Streets on the Dallas-to-Denison line. This was about ten years after the city of East Dallas merged into the present city of Dallas in 1890. Highland Park Shopping Center was

Before the advent of suburban shopping centers, in the early twentieth century Dallasites did their shopping at neighborhood stores such as the E. Tabor Grocery Store on Santa Fe Street in East Dallas. Note the milk cow in front of the Tabor's Victorian style home which provided the family with milk and butter, a practice rather common as Dallas made the change from rural to urban lifestyle.

Dallas County's first "off the street" shopping center and one of the first of its kind in America. It was built after 1929.

Dallas can thank a present-day rival for its security. In its infancy the small village of Dallas was plagued by dangerous and costly raids by Indians who lived in what is now the shadows of Dallas' skyscrapers. Security from such raids was provided by the building of Camp Worth, which became Fort Worth.

The early transit system linking Dallas with Oak Cliff was highly advertised as "The first elevated railway in the South." But the "elevated" actually ran at ground level on both the Dallas and Oak Cliff sides. Only the trestle and bridge that spanned the river channel and flood plain was elevated.

During a celebration of the end of World War I in November of 1918, a Lt. Bottrell broke his own record for highest parachute jump. The record was 6,000 feet in 1918, and Bottrell jumped from 7,000 feet, landing before spectators at Love Field in Dallas.

Belle Starr Drive is a street in the Pleasant Grove area of Dallas near St. Augustine Road. This location is approximately where the old town of Scyene was, the hometown of the "Outlaw Queen of Indian Territory."

Thousands of commuters stream past the corner of Interstate 30 (old Highway 80) and Gus Thomasson Road daily without being aware that this location was once the town of Truman, Texas, now a part of Mesquite. It is safe to say that only a handful of people in that city know about Truman, with the exception of the few former residents of Truman and a few public officials. The story of Truman is a simple one and typical of many small communities with a heart and a history that were gobbled up by larger cities with better capability to serve their residents. While the name may be lost, the story of the town of Truman is worth passing on to those with an interest in preserving our heritage. According to newspaper clippings, on November 21, 1945, Mrs. E.H. Hopkins christened the town of Truman into existence with a milk bottle. She was quoted as saying that the reason she used a bottle of milk was "because so many of the community's residents were Baptists." The sign she christened read "Dallas city limits 7 miles." The dedication included the reading of numerous letters of congratulations, and Dallas postmaster J. Howard Payne read a telegram from President Harry Truman stating, "I am deeply conscious of the honor which the new community in Dallas County is according me in giving my name to the town of Truman. I send my hearty felicitations and warmest personal greetings to all of the townspeople—Harry S. Truman." The community had been called by at least six other names prior to being named Truman: Chitlin Switch, The Gravy, Deanville, North Mesquite, and Mesquite Tap. The trading post owned by E.C. Cogburn was the stop for a bus line which called the place Mesquite Tap before it became Truman. The community had a population of about 200 with several businesses and a church. Mrs. Hopkins, the self-appointed historian of Truman, said in an interview that "there were only eight telephone lines in the area, and when your phone would ring the eight-phone party line would listen in." The main reason the community incorporated in the first place was in an attempt to get water, telephone, and utility service. Truman had no post office, and requests for letters to receive a Truman postmark couldn't be met. The first mail in Truman was marked RFD and delivered by Jack McDonald, who was a champion cross-country bicycle rider. Although the town honoring the president received a lot of national attention, including a write-up in *Time Magazine*, it was soon annexed into Mesquite. But according to the Mesquite Public Library, there are still a few homes that date from when the town was Truman.

```
                    DB77
D.WB533 N  D. WB533  NL  GOVT  PD WASHINGTON  DC 20
  J HOWARD PAINE▪
          POSTMASTER  DAL▪

I AM DEEPLY CONSCIOUS OF THE HONOR WHICH THE NEW COMMINITY IN
DALLAS COUNTY IS ACÇORDING ME IN GIVING MY NAME TO THE TOWN
OF TRUMAN. I SEND HEARTY FELICIATIONS AND WARMEST PERSONAL
GREETINGS TO ALL OF THE TOWNSPEOPLE▪
          HARRY  S  TRUMAN..
```

A figure known from Amarillo to Brownsville, from Waskom to El Paso, and all points in between is the Texas State Fair's goodwill ambassador, Big Tex. The 52-foot-tall cowboy who has greeted visitors to the fair since 1952 commands attention with his immense boots

and friendly "Howdyeeee folks! Welcome to the State
Fair of Texas...." For more than three decades Big Tex's
friendly voice has been provided by Dallas radio
personality Jim Lowe. But though many can't imagine
Big Tex as anything other than the friendly giant cowboy,
the big guy started out in life as jolly ol' Saint Nick in
the small but ambitious Navarro County town of Kerens.
Nora Lee May of the Chamber of Commerce was one of
the many volunteers in 1949 who helped create the
"Largest Santa Claus in the World," unraveling hemp
rope to make his giant Santa beard. According to May,
creating the giant Santa was the idea of Chamber
manager Howell Brister, who thought it would be a
stimulus to business for the merchants of Kerens. Brister,
according to a story in the December 24, 1978, issue of
the *Corsicana Daily Sun,* "was concerned with getting
local people to stay and shop at home in the post-World
War II years. Brister felt he had to do something big to
do it, and that is how he got the idea to build 'the
world's largest Santa Claus.' Not only would it keep
Kerens' people at home trading with local merchants, it
would attract more than a few visitors from around the
country, out of curiosity, who might spend a few dollars."
Brister was quoted as saying that he went to Dallas and
bought 168 yards of red oilcloth, and employees at the
Kerens dress factory, in their after-work time, cut and
stitched Santa's suit together. May said some of the men
donated material, and boys from Roy Cloud's vocational
agriculture class helped construct the jolly ol' elf's frame.
The giant Santa served the town well for two years.
Quite visible, he towered over the town from where he
stood on Colket Street, the main street of Kerens. When
Cotton Belt trains stopped in town, passengers, alerted
by conductors, would get off the train to look at the
immense figure. But alas, Santa's stay in Kerens came to

an end when he was blown down by a wind storm.
Brister convinced the Chamber to sell Santa to some
small West Texas town where maybe he could do some
good for them as he had for Kerens. He set out by car to
sell Santa for $1,000 with the chimney that had been
built around him the second year or $750 without the
chimney. On the way he stopped at the State Fair of
Texas' offices, and after seeing a large color photograph
of Santa, State Fair manager James Stewart and
president R.L. "Uncle Bob" Thornton bought Santa for
$750. After a year Santa made his debut as Big Tex,
trading his stocking cap for a ten-gallon hat. This tallest
of Texans has a neck more than twelve feet in diameter.
His cotton shirt is made of 129 yards of fabric, enough
to make more than forty regular shirts. Manufacturing
attire for the jovial giant is somewhat as challenging as
making a saddle for Dallas' flying red horse! According to
May, when she comes to the State Fair she can squint her
eyes and look at Big Tex and still see Santa. Big Tex paid
one last visit to Kerens during the town's centennial in
1981, a move that required much planning and labor.
Although he returned as Big Tex and not Santa, those of
Kerens' citizens who remembered him from their
childhood no doubt saw a little of the jolly ol' elf in him.

Index

189